CANDIDATES PRAISE
THE RIGHT FIT METHOD

A candidate who asked not to receive his offer:

My first thought when I spoke with Dr. Arlene Barro for the first time was, "Who is this woman?" A complete stranger, she had called me to talk about an open position she thought I might be right for. She hinted that my résumé would need updating, even before she'd seen it, and that I'd need interview coaching, even though she'd never interviewed me. I was an adult, and, in my opinion, my résumé was perfectly fine. And I knew I was perfectly comfortable in interview situations, thank you very much.

But her enchanting personality got the best of me—that and the fact that the position in question was a fabulous one in a unique organization. After spending two hours having my résumé pulled apart, I saw she had a point. After another two hours of interview coaching, I realized I had been transformed. Arlene didn't want to repackage me so she could pull the wool over the employer's eyes, make the sale, and get me the job. Instead, she wanted me to pay careful attention to her two candidate mantras: "Manage the Process" and "Probe."

As a candidate you mustn't just sit in an interview and field questions that employers throw at you. You have to set the pace and the course of the discussion yourself. And when you probe, you can, as I did, find something out about the employer that the employer doesn't even know. Armed with that knowledge, you can level the playing field and assess each other as equals. In the end, based on the information I uncovered, I decided that I didn't want Dr. Barro to extend an offer to me on the employer's behalf.

I dreaded telling her; she had spent many hours with me. But to my surprise, she simply listened, asked if I was absolutely sure, then made no protest. We chatted for a while, and then she wished me well. Her goal wasn't to squeeze me into the job; it was to make a perfect match.

She believes no match is better than a bad match, and this is a testament to the power of her process. Most important of all, Arlene understood that her hours were not a waste of time. I had graduated; I'd learned enough about myself and about the process to liberate myself. I used my newfound wisdom to find on my own the position I truly wanted and that I was right for, and I use it still from the other side of the table when I talk with and interview candidates. I would have never reached this level of awareness without Arlene. Once you graduate, you never forget.

A candidate who was offered her choice of three positions by an employer:

What a remarkable experience it was for me to be evaluated and coached by Dr. Arlene Barro in preparation for my meeting with the prospective employer for whom she believed I was the Right Fit. We spoke in great depth as we prepared for my interview; it was like having a career personal trainer by my side. Throughout the process, she was there to ensure that things were progressing smoothly. Thanks to Dr. Barro, I was so well prepared that her client not only wanted to hire me, but presented a choice of three positions. My choice was a position the company created specifically for me. Dr. Barro extended the offer to me, and I allowed her to accept on my behalf. How exhilarating it was, and how grateful I am for her counsel and support.

REVIEWERS' APPLAUSE FOR
WIN WITHOUT COMPETING!

"*Win Without Competing!* sets a standard against which no one can compete. Understanding all the players, Dr. Barro—in a supportive, nurturing, and inspiring style—presents a convincing argument for her Right Fit Method, a career search tool that enables all sides to win.

In my experience, both in recruiting talent and in my own professional career, identifying the Right Fit is the key. If equal energy were applied to identifying the right position, the right company, and the right talent, resources would not be wasted and better outcomes would be achieved.

I recommend taking the time to implement the Right Fit Method not only during your career search but also throughout your life. I envision candidates, employees, entrepreneurs, employers, and human resources professionals using the Right Fit Method and achieving stellar results."

—*Lourdes M. Hassler*, MBA, CEO,
National Society of Hispanic MBAs

(see more on next page)

REVIEWERS' APPLAUSE FOR
WIN WITHOUT COMPETING!

"Dr. Barro really puts forward a very compelling approach to attaining personal success and satisfaction not only in your job but also in your life. As exemplified in the career journeys of her 'storytellers,' her Right Fit Method works both for recruiters and for those seeking to attain their full career potential. As a result, her book *Win Without Competing!* is a must reference source for job seekers and human resources professionals in every field. Importantly, Dr. Barro's writing style makes the book entertaining reading."

 —*John W. Fara*, PhD, Chairman and CEO, Depomed, Inc.

"*Win Without Competing!* lays out Dr. Arlene Barro's innovative approach to both finding the right position and hiring Right Fit candidates in a clear, insightful, step-by-step manner. I worked with Dr. Barro on a key hire and have seen her Right Fit Method in action. Reading the book gave me additional insights into hiring and managing talented people without the guesswork. *Win Without Competing!* is an essential read, whether you're an employer searching for the right employee, an individual searching for the right position, or simply a person looking to reach your potential in an existing one."

 —*Jim Sexton*, Senior Vice President,
 Interactive Brands, Scripps Networks

WIN
WITHOUT
COMPETING!

Career Success the **RIGHT FIT** *Way*

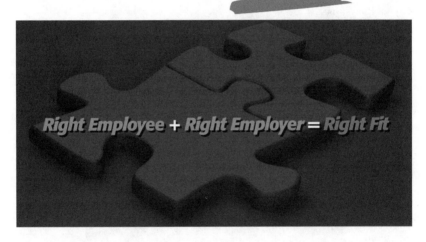

Right Employee + Right Employer = Right Fit

Arlene R. Barro, PhD

Capital Books, Inc.
P.O. Box 605
Herndon, Virginia 20172-0605

Note: Original purchasers of this book are permitted to photocopy forms in this book for personal use only, not for distribution.

ISBN: 978-1-933102-38-2

Library of Congress Cataloging-in-Publication Data
Barro, Arlene R.
Win without competing! : career success the right fit way / Arlene R. Barro.
p. cm. — (Capital ideas for business & personal development series)
Includes index.
ISBN-13: 978-1-933102-38-2 (alk. paper)
1. Career development. 2. Success in business. 3. Employees—Recruiting.
4. Employee selection. I. Title.
HF5381.B323 2007
650.1—dc22
2007014579

Printed in the United States of America on acid-free paper that meets the American National Standards Institute Z39-48 Standard.

First Edition

10 9 8 7 6 5 4 3 2 1

WIN
WITHOUT
COMPETING!

Career Success the **RIGHT FIT** *Way*

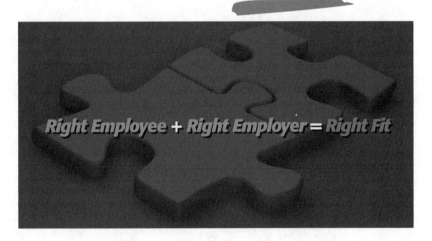

Right Employee + *Right Employer* = *Right Fit*

Arlene R. Barro, PhD

Capital Books, Inc.
Sterling, Virginia

CAPITAL
BOOKS, INC.

To *my dad,*

Cantor Tevelle H. Ring,

who taught me to listen intently to what people say
—merging heart, mind, and soul—
to experience the essence of who they are.

Confucius said,
CHOOSE A JOB YOU LOVE, AND
YOU WILL NEVER HAVE TO WORK
A DAY IN YOUR LIFE,
and what was true in his time remains
oh, so true today.

CONTENTS

FOREWORD

I MET ARLENE BARRO by phone in the sweltering Atlanta summer of 1998. I was involved in a launch of a massive health web site that would eventually become the juggernaut now known as webmd.com with 31 million monthly visitors. I was the editor-in-chief, and the chairman had handed me the job of launching thirty channels of comprehensive, accurate, credible content for the general public, for physicians, and for nurses.

With that kind of deadline, you cannot recruit great candidates on your own. You need help. That's when Arlene Barro rode into my life on her white horse. She was the Right Fit at exactly the right time for WebMD's establishment and growth.

Over the first few weeks, Dr. Barro walked me through her method, which she had named the Right Fit. We talked at great length and arrived at a blueprint of the Right Fit for different positions that were open. I was looking for doctors, nurses, writers, editors, and, in one case, a division president outside the United States. Over the next two years, I hired forty candidates from Dr. Barro, my exclusive search consultant. She filled the openings on my staff in three countries. The Right Fit Method worked for WebMD's growth in the United States, the United Kingdom, and Canada. I couldn't believe that almost every candidate she presented to me was, in fact, the Right Fit. I didn't need to see lots of candidates and select the "best" among them, and I saved an enormous amount of time. With Dr. Barro's help, we were able to find and hire high-level personnel. Without those Right Fit candidates, I would not have been successful. The quality and character of the hires matched my blueprint for growth plans extremely well. Together, we built WebMD to its current status as the Internet's most visited healthcare site with 230 million page views per month.

I've had the good fortune to have read the early drafts of *Win Without Competing!*, and I have read with great pleasure this unique, innovative, and challenging business-career book. It teaches candidates and employees how to implement the Right Fit Method step-by-step. At the same time, they can peek into the minds of employers and get a valuable sense of how those executives think and act. The result: Candidates learn how to make the most of a proven method for career success. And employers learn how to use the Right Fit Method to hire perfect candidates and save time and money, as I did, seldom needing to fire and re-hire. They do it right the first time when they're armed with the Right Fit Method. For everyone on both sides of the table, strategy replaces stress—the Right Fit Way.

I highly recommend *Win Without Competing!* to candidates, employees, and employers.

Tom Lombardo
Founding Editor-in-Chief
WebMD

ACKNOWLEDGMENTS

DRAWING FROM MY OWN CAREER experiences as a search consultant and career coach, I have woven a rich tapestry of stories to illustrate the concept, implementation, and benefits of the Right Fit Method. I want to thank my candidates, employees, and my client-employers for permitting me to test and prove this new way of identifying, hiring, and retaining the Right Fit employee for the Right Fit employer.

To my storytellers, I thank you and admire you for your candor. You shared your professional and personal stories, with one goal in mind—to enlighten the reader. I'm grateful to:

Tom Lombardo, who shared, in one sentence, the secret of good writing, which I immediately implemented;

Ashton Clarke Rice, for patiently deciphering more than 70,000 handwritten words and meticulously and flawlessly typing my manuscript;

Russell Martin, who polished my pearls, understood my Right Fit Method, and added the right touches to enhance the message; and

Danny Fausto and Russell Robinson for designing the Packaged to Pitch logo to match the concept.

My heartfelt thanks to Marc Kusinitz, Joe Ortiz, and Patti Rager, who read drafts of my manuscript and responded with excitement, encouragement, and praise.

Thank you to Joelle Delbourgo, my literary agent, who introduced me to Kathleen Hughes, the Right Fit publisher who recognized, appreciated, and reinforced my creativity, showing me the impact of subtle changes.

Special thanks to the mistress of the devil's details, Amy Fries, editor extraordinaire, Capital Books.

To you, the reader, my everlasting thanks for participating with me on a journey that can dramatically change your professional and personal life.

Away we go!

Arlene R. Barro, PhD

PROLOGUE

TOGETHER, WE ARE about to attend a performance that will change your life forever. It's titled "Win Without Competing." Its actors will demonstrate on stage the Right Fit Method, which I created to enable them—and *you*—to succeed in their professional and personal lives without competing against each other.

During the production, you will meet a wide array of people on the stage, some of whom successfully Win Without Competing, and others who do not. You will meet Jason, Patti, and Ned, who are major characters in this drama. They are real people who play out their stories specifically for you, revealing their inner selves to illustrate how truly life-changing it can be when you Win Without Competing. You will meet other characters as well, some of whom have difficulty succeeding in their professional and personal lives because they have not yet learned how to let go of competing against others and focus instead on finding the Right Fit. Many of the players' names are their own. I've changed the names of others in order to protect their need for privacy.

As the storytellers reveal themselves, no doubt you will see elements of yourself in them, something that will help you understand yourself better. You will experience a broad range of emotions as you explore who you are and determine who you want to be. Gradually, you will change how you view yourself as well as how you view others around you. You will learn how to step back and view yourself as others see you—as if you too were on that stage.

As the production's creator and narrator, I comment on the storytellers' stories as well as share stories from my own professional and personal life. And I use the interwoven stories to teach you how to implement my Right Fit Method as the solution to your career and personal dilemmas.

In the end, you are the central character in this drama. The narrator and storytellers have no greater goal than to demonstrate the effectiveness of this new way of thinking and acting. Your enthusiastic participation is vital. You, the storytellers, and I will create a performance unlike any other, and we have no time to waste. I welcome you to this exciting production and thank you for your interest in learning how you can change every aspect of your professional and personal life for the better when you Win Without Competing.

Arlene R. Barro, PhD

A DRAMA IN FOUR ACTS

ACT I

Setting the Stage

INTRODUCTION

Win Without Competing!

You are holding something revolutionary in your hands. It's a book unlike any other you have read, one that will help you become a career-strategy expert who is no longer forced to compete to win, and the kind of business professional who successfully achieves every one of the goals you set. Win Without Competing! *will provide you with step-by-step solutions and enable you to adopt new career strategies that will change your life. I invite you to join me on a remarkable journey.*

BELIEVE ME, I RECOGNIZE what a daunting dilemma it is not to know where you want to go with your career. It's also enormously frustrating to have a clear vision of where you want to go, yet not know how to get there, particularly if you've devoted years and resources to a specific career path. Most of us need help in moving toward the lives we were meant to lead, but finding the right mentors and coaches is far from simple. You need someone who understands you, your dreams and desires, your strengths and weaknesses on the one hand, and the world of business and its often-labyrinthine hiring processes on the other. You need someone who can help flatten the fears generated by career crises and the decisions they demand, someone who provides psychological support as well as the critical tools that move you toward a position to which you're perfectly suited and in which you soar.

I'm an educator who understands the keys to making learning easy and enjoyable, an educational psychologist adept at empowering change, and an evaluator who can show you how to analyze your career and how best to move it forward. I spent many years in high-level educational healthcare management positions before I became an entrepreneur, founding and still leading my company—barro global search, inc. Early in my search career, I created the groundbreaking system I'll introduce to you here. By the time you finish reading *Win Without Competing!* you'll be able to skillfully implement my system, one that I trust will become your constant lifetime companion.

If you'll take my lessons to heart and open yourself to real and substantive change, we can achieve great things, you and I. In the chapters that follow, I'll take you on a fascinating tour of the career marketplace. I'll point out and set you free from an array of faulty assumptions, the most poisonous of which is the belief—shared by thousands of candidates, employees, and employers—that career success is dependent on competition. *It is not*, and the sooner you can shed the competition mind-set, the easier it will be for you to succeed in profoundly new and satisfying ways.

The truth is that our culture has wrongly led us to believe that we always should ask comparison questions: What's the best movie? The best car? The best college for our kids? The problem with that approach is that it presumes that there is a single and identifiable "best," when, in fact, "best" is utterly dependent on related criteria: Best for whom? Best for achieving what goals? Best for how long? I've learned to ask a completely different question, one that is radical and life-changing, yet at the same time wonderfully straightforward. My fundamental question is founded on standards or criteria; it's utterly focused on finding what I call the Right Fit. I never concern myself with which position is "best" for a candidate, or which candidate is "best" for a particular employer, because I've found a far better way. *My* sole *concern is finding an exquisite fit between the two—like the interlocking pieces of a puzzle.*

I approach my work in a unique way, quite unlike the methods of other search and placement firms in the United States. When I conduct a search for an employer, I spend many critically important hours listening, researching, and asking questions before creating a protocol or "blueprint" comprising detailed specifications for the open position and its ideal candidate. Then I work tirelessly to find the person who precisely fits that blueprint, and eventually I present that candidate to the employer. I never offer an array of choices because there is no need to do so; the employer and I aren't judging the "best" of many candidates, after all; we're simply in search of the Right Fit. And that's the key to my success—and to yours.

My Right Fit Method is strategic, creative, and one-of-a-kind, and it's a system that *works*. Sure, some client-employers who've never retained me before are skeptical, even quite nervous, as we begin the process, but invariably they love the approach and trust me implicitly by the time we've completed our mission. Why? Because the employers I work with save *lots* of time—there are no year-long searches in my world, as are commonplace with other search firms who present an array of candidates. The standard but so-often unsuccessful system of comparing candidates leads to hiring—and then firing—the wrong person because the employers pay too little attention in the first place to how well the candidate matches the position and the institutional culture of the organization. My clients, on the other hand, rarely fire employees I've placed with them, nor do those employees leave—simply because we ensure the Right Fit from the outset.

And what do my search and coaching candidates think of my approach? It's a dream come true, they'll tell you. They love turning their backs to the warrior mind-set that insists they are in a fight to the finish with every other person interested in the same position. My search candidates love the fact that I present them without competing candidates. My coaching candidates trust that there is a situation out there to which they are perfectly suited; and when we find it together, they begin that new career opportunity secure in the knowledge that they fit it perfectly, and that it will lead to a long, fruitful, and mutually supportive relationship with their employer.

In the Right Fit Method, we understand that when you eliminate comparison, you eliminate competition against others while still achieving your goals—every time. *In the Right Fit Method, we forget about the "best" and focus instead on finding the perfect match.* As you and I proceed, you'll learn how to use this breakthrough approach to shape, sell, and share your Personal Brand—the compelling professional identity you present to the employer with whom you've carefully determined you want to work—and in doing so, how to move your career and your life forward in dramatic new ways.

Instead of focusing on your competitors, you will focus on yourself. You will learn how to implement my Right Fit Method to *set a standard against which no one can compete.* If you're saying, "I don't know what my next career step should be," worry not. I will show you how to find your Core Identity right now. If you're trying to figure out how to balance your professional and personal lives in relation to each other, as well as create the Right Fit personal life for yourself, you will have the tools to do so. Mastering and implementing my Right Fit Method daily will make you feel fulfilled, both professionally and personally.

Our society is in a state of constant change, and so are our careers, which affect our personal lives. Each of us must always be ready—and very willing—to open one door as we close another. If today you're employed, tomorrow you may be downsized; or perhaps you realize you're decidedly the *wrong fit* in your current position and are considering making a change. If you're dissatisfied in any way, the good news is that if you have the courage and dedication to open those doors, and if you educate yourself about the true dynamics of the employee-employer relationship and how to dramatically manage them in your favor, you can transform a currently unacceptable situation into a welcome opportunity for career growth.

What do employers think of my approach? As my former client-employer Tom Lombardo described in the book's foreword, I successfully placed *forty* candidates with him during the time he was the founding editor-in-chief of the hugely successful online health-information site WebMD. Each of those people who joined Tom's team in the United States, Canada, and the United Kingdom was the Right Fit for the exciting new venture they collectively undertook. Tom vows never to hire anyone again without employing the Right Fit Method. Like him, decision makers and human resources professionals who implement my system can hire candidates faster, significantly reducing hiring mistakes, and eliminating the need to fire or repeat searches because the wrong-fit person was hired. Applying the Right Fit Method to evaluate employees can dramatically reduce unproductive inter-employee competition and foster organization-wide support and goodwill.

Candidates who read *Win Without Competing!* and commit to making the changes I recommend can successfully position themselves on the right career paths for themselves; they will know how to effectively manage unexpected career events to achieve what *they* desire, not what others choose for them. They become confident and in charge of their futures, unafraid of failure, ready to launch targeted campaigns to capture the right position.

It's a promise I proudly make: *Win Without Competing!* will alter forever the way you look at the too-often daunting world of search and placement. In the new millennium, we're no longer bound by the methods and practices of the past, particularly when fresh strategies can replace the dog-eat-dog approach to hiring and career management and when sane, civilized, and *successful* new systems offer such a welcome alternative. In the new millennium, we can eliminate comparison and thereby end destructive competition, and everyone can thrive. I've seen my system work for more than a decade, and I'm eager to share it with you.

Frequently Asked Questions about The Right Fit Method

Q: Can the Right Fit Method be implemented to secure positions in all industries?

A: Yes, the Method is applicable to all industries.

Q: Is it suitable for new grads and young professionals?

A: Yes, the Method provides the roadmap to achieve career success early in life, with minimal need to change learned behaviors. It teaches young professionals how to overcome objections to minimal or no experience.

Q: Is it applicable to entrepreneurs?

A: Yes. With the tools of the Right Fit Method, entrepreneurs can dramatically build their client base and hire—and retain—Right Fit employees and/or independent contractors.

Q: Is it right for employees in all stages, phases, and levels of their careers?

A: Yes, each of these employee situations can be successfully addressed with the Method: You're eager to be promoted, but don't know how to proceed. You're unhappy and don't know whether you should fix your situation or flee. Awaiting downsizing, you're nervous and you need a plan. Downsized but still employed, you anticipate being jobless and respond with an ineffective résumé blast.

Q: Is it effective for the unemployed?

A: Yes—it is not uncommon for people who are unemployed to remain "in transition" for a year or more. They need a holistic, supportive system, one that is founded on their Core Identity, which, for many, is difficult to identify.

Q: Is it valuable for employers?

A: Yes, the Method is particularly valuable for employers in small businesses without HR departments but with critical needs for Right Fit employees; for medium-sized businesses that need Right Fit employees to grow; and for large businesses that spend too much time hiring, firing, and rehiring. ■

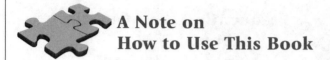

A Note on
How to Use This Book

Win Without Competing! is presented in four major acts:

- Setting the Stage (Warming Up)
- How the Right Fit Method Works (Nuts and Bolts)
- Applying the Right Fit Method (Let's Do It!)
- The Right Fit Method and You

The first three acts focus on your professional life, and the fourth on your personal life. Imagine achieving total balance—your professional life in relation to your personal—finally finding the road to happiness and leaving the stress behind you.

I know it can be tempting to skip from chapter to chapter when you read. However, in this case it's vitally important to read this book systematically, from beginning to end. Then I suggest re-reading those chapters and sections that are a particular Right Fit for you at the appropriate time.

The chapters include a variety of tools to help you get the most out of your reading:

- Your goal for that chapter,
- Activities to help you achieve that goal,
- An activities journal in which to record your performance and progress,
- Storytellers, real people who share their stories on a stage,
- Employers' perspective on hiring, downsizing, and firing, based on my professional experience,
- A Trigger Tip to help you recall and reinforce your goal.

Together, let's begin our journey now.

CHAPTER ONE

The Concept of the Right Fit Method

Your Goal:
Forget the Competition!

Nᴏᴛ ʟᴏɴɢ ᴀɢᴏ, a very talented young woman named Barbara called me, hoping I could coach her. She introduced herself by saying, "I am a lawyer and a second-year MBA candidate at the Wharton School. I enjoy the world of business law . . . but I don't want to simply bury my head in documents for the rest of my career." I could hear the urgency in Barbara' voice and asked her to tell me more. Her credentials were da zling—a BA with honors from UCLA, near where she v raised, a law degree from Stanford, and soon she would the MBA from Wharton to her résumé. At age thirty-one already had led the research team of a prestigious San cisco law firm on several large real-estate cases.

"Barbara," I said, "describe your dream position

"I can't visualize the exact job I want," she responded, "but I know it's out there. Can you help me?"

I explained to Barbara that I could help her if she were willing to examine her Core Identity. Her remarkable background was wonderful, but she didn't know who she was as a professional or what she wanted to do with her career. Before searching for the right career position, we decided to work together, first to identify her Core Identity and then to match the Right Fit position to her new Core Identity. Shortly, I will tell you more about Barbara.

As a career coach and search and placement consultant working with candidates from around the country, I meet many people who are at career crossroads, yet who don't know how to successfully move themselves forward. Some, like Barbara, simply aren't sure which career path they want to embark on; others suffer from burn-out and seek more creative satisfaction in their lives; and thousands more have been caught in the downsizing that accompanied the nation's dramatic economic downturn, finding themselves unemployed and uncertain about their futures. I know downsized, high-level managers from all industries who have spent thousands of dollars with outplacement firms in years-long searches for new positions—sometimes in vain, despite the enormous investment. Increasingly, career professionals are forced, often in middle-age, to re-imagine and re-make themselves in hopes of thriving again, a task that can be incredibly daunting, particularly because a career candidate who doesn't know how to successfully market him or herself will never be interviewed and has no chance of ever being hired.

As fears and frustrations mount, confidence levels decline; many people accept whatever is offered to them simply because they *have* to have employment and the income it provides. They don't advance—staying stuck and remaining unhappy and unfulfilled—or they don't last, quitting if they aren't fired first. My long experience has taught me that most candidates, even the most highly qualified professionals, consistently make three critical mistakes that prevent them from being invited to interview:

- First, like Barbara, they fail to accurately evaluate their dreams and desires together with their technical and interpersonal skills to determine what positions match their capabilities and in what positions they believe they can thrive. *It's absolutely essential to investigate, study, and soul-search to determine the right career path to follow before investing many years of training for a particular profession, only to discover that it's not for you.*

- Second, instead of evaluating themselves, they take a shotgun approach to their dilemma, blasting cyberspace with e-mailed résumés, hoping someone, somewhere will notice them, then hire them.

- Third, they fail to compare the specifications of a position posting with their backgrounds and skills to determine whether they and the opportunity are, in fact, a great match. I know all too well from working with professionals that downsized software engineers often apply for teaching positions, and that out-of-work physicians sometimes seek director-of nursing-slots—situations for which they are *not* perfect matches, and which, almost certainly, they will not be offered.

To hear an employer say, "You're hired," for a position to which you're terrifically well-suited—and in which you'll be happy and successful—requires the creation and implementation of a well-designed and vigorously executed campaign, every bit as much as if you were running for elective office. *Win Without Competing!* is my detailed plan for that campaign—how to conceive it in ways that maximize its potential for success, how to set it in motion and sustain it over time, and how to ensure the "victory" that is the best possible fit between you and a position you'll love.

Books that stress how to compete against other candidates successfully focus on what's known as *normative-reference measurement*, the comparing of candidates against each other as they vie for a particular position. Employers around the country can't imagine approaching the task of hiring any other way: *Who is the best we have among our sea of applicants? Let's see who is the cream that rises to the top.* Often, a shockingly small amount of attention is paid to the actual needs of the company or organization, and to whom, in fact, can best meet them.

But there is another way—a far better way. It's an approach that's based on what I call *criterion-reference measurement*, the comparing of candidates for a particular position not with each other but rather with a carefully constructed blueprint of the position, which includes the ideal qualifications of the individual who will fill it. In my system, the focus is *always* on matching skills, abilities, training, and experience to specific criteria, which are the essential components of the Right Fit between the individual (who is the seller, after all) and the organization or employer (the buyer).

Normative-reference measurement makes great sense when you're buying tomatoes—you want the very best tomatoes in the bin, don't you?—but when you're buying the services of someone who will become a trusted colleague and invaluable co-worker, simply looking for who's "best" runs the real and constant risk that the "best" candidate isn't at all suited to the position in question. Over the years, I've succeeded in training my client-employers to use my criterion-reference measurement system instead, and once they've mastered it, not one of them has ever wanted to revert to the old, outmoded, and so often unsuccessful direct-competition approach to hiring. In *Win Without Competing!*, I'll teach you how to employ criterion-reference measurement in managing your career and more—you'll also learn how to influence the decision makers with whom you interview to do the same. As they do, you'll gain critical insights into the perspectives, limitations, and desires of the organizations you're eager to join.

Let's look at Barbara's situation to demonstrate how the Right Fit Method works. What should she do first on the path toward realizing her goal of being offered a great position in which she will be rewarded in every way?

The *RIGHT FIT* Method

THE CORE IDENTITY

THE PERSONAL BRAND
- The Right Fit
- Package to Pitch
- Manage the Process

THE CALCULATED CLOSE

THE TOTAL PACKAGE

The Core Identity

Before she does *anything* else, it's critical for Barbara to spend time defining her Core Identity—what are the professional competencies, personality, and goals with which she defines herself and creates her career path? Does she decide to continue pursuing the career in real-estate law that her JD and MBA have prepared her for? Would a career in another area of law better suit her? Does she want to work for herself, rather than a large firm? Let's imagine that after much consideration, family input, and self-analysis using my Core Identity system, Barbara ultimately determines that what she truly seeks is a career in entertainment law. She grew up in southern California, where her father was a network television executive. She's always been fascinated by the worlds of film and television, knows that lawyers in the entertainment field often work in small, boutique-style firms, and that their daily lives involve constant interaction with dynamic and innovative people.

We used my Core Identity System to analyze her Core Identity. Barbara was delighted to learn that her Core Identity as a lawyer was correct, but that she needed to change the industry in which she should practice law. Implementing her new balanced Core Identity, Barbara would seek a position in entertainment.

Her next step is to create a "roadmap" that will lead her toward the successful implementation of her balanced Core Identity—in her particular case, comprehensively branding herself as someone who is expertly schooled in both law and business and who has a keen understanding of the many challenges and opportunities of the entertainment world. And it's only after Barbara determines and can truly articulate her balanced Core Identity that she begins to look for the right position at a small entertainment-focused firm.

Barbara is now ready to create her Personal Brand, which is the professional identity she will carefully tailor to the position she seeks. To do this, she will determine the Right Fit, Package herself to Pitch, and Manage the Process. Let's see how this works.

The Right Fit

Once she identifies an opportunity which, on its surface at least, seems attractive and just might be one she wants to vigorously pursue, Barbara develops what I call a blueprint of the stated specifications for the advertised position. She researches the firm, its decision makers, its successes in the industry, and as much other information as she can possibly glean. When that extensive task is completed, she next matches her own specs to the blueprint to see whether the two appear to form a good fit—the Right Fit.

Barbara conducts a preliminary evaluation to assess her fit with the position. If Barbara determines that her specs match at 80 percent or better with the blueprint, then she needs to verify the fit, which requires contacting the employer. If the match is less than 80 percent, she abandons that particular possibility and looks for another open position. But let's say that in this case, Barbara matches 80 percent of the blueprint criteria and calls the employer to obtain more information to verify the fit. If she confirms that the fit is at 80 percent or more, Barbara will then create her Right Fit résumé. If she finds out that the fit is wrong, she does not proceed.

Let's say the fit is right and she proceeds. She drafts, revises, and polishes her Right Fit résumé to make herself fit the position as close to 100 percent as she can, carefully articulating her match to the position specs. Barbara has now completed the first major step.

Package to Pitch

The second major step, one I call Package to Pitch, is an examination and articulation of the Right Fit, a broadcast that Barbara has fashioned to communicate how she fits the blueprint for the position she seeks. It's an essential step that requires practice, insight, eloquence, and brimming self-confidence; when Barbara has accomplished it successfully, she is ready for her interview.

Manage the Process

Now it's time for Barbara to implement the third major step in creating her personal brand—Manage the Process—and to articulate her broadcast (Package to Pitch). When she meets with the two partners at the small Hollywood firm she hopes to work for, it is Barbara who takes charge of the interview, powerfully articulating the Right Fit she's fashioned between herself and the opportunity. She keeps the interviewers focused solely on criterion-reference measurement—evaluating her against the set of standards they created. She never discusses why she's "the best person for the job." Instead she repeatedly highlights for the firm's partners how remarkably well her skills, training, and experience match their needs and the specifications they have created for the position.

The Calculated Close

At each stage along the way, Barbara also has paid careful attention to an essential component of the system that I call the Calculated Close, a series of steps that ensure that she and her prospective employers are moving in unison toward an offer that includes the most comprehensive package possible. Issues such as her compensation, partnership potential, relocation, benefits, office, and whether she'll have the ability to hire her own assistant have been openly raised, discussed, and preliminarily negotiated during the days leading up to this point.

Not bedeviled by the details, but rather keenly attuned to them, Barbara has a clear and comfortable understanding of the parameters of the offer well before it's presented, virtually eliminating the need to negotiate further once the offer is formally on the table—an offer that, ultimately, delights her.

Barbara has self-directed her way to a position that will allow her to thrive, one in which her remarkable talents and experience will be highly utilized and greatly appreciated, a situation in the entertainment field in which she'll remain satisfied for a long time, a position she's proud to hold.

The Total Package

Someone once remarked that I am "constantly closing." And it's an apt characterization. I never wait until I'm concluding anything to start closing. What am I really doing? *I'm setting a standard against which no one can compete.*

When I'm conducting a search or coaching a candidate, I focus on meeting and exceeding expectations. If you do the same, paying careful attention to the devil's details, you will set a similar standard against which no one can compete. But keep in mind that sometimes it's very clear what's missing in the Total Package. Often, however, it is not.

For example, I once had a candidate who lost an offer for a CPA position because she wore her sunglasses on her head throughout her interview. In the end, her prospective employer didn't care that she perfectly matched his specs. All he could remember when he debriefed me was those sunglasses, perched where he didn't think they belonged.

I ultimately placed the candidate with another client-employer, but I can assure you, she'll never wear her sunglasses into a meeting or interview again.

It's details like that one that ultimately will determine whether you receive an offer or only a dismissive "we wish you the best" comment as you are turned away. And it's only one of many details I'll share with you as we continue our journey together.

Why was Barbara successful in implementing the Right Fit Method?

A key component that led to Barbara's success was her ability to change her behavior, particularly her old habit of making assumptions. Over and over, she had to learn to do things quite differently from the ways she was used to.

Reflecting on my conversation with Barbara, I remember carefully listening to her voice. She spoke with some hesitation, which surprised me. Several times, I had to ask her to speak louder. I reminded myself not to make assumptions and probed to find out why her confidence level did not match her credentials. I found out that her father had recently died and she was depressed. He had been her career mentor. Now, she had no one with whom to discuss her career dilemma, and that was what had motivated Barbara to contact me. I explained the Right Fit Method to her, and she decided that it sounded like the Right Fit for her. I asked her a series of questions to assess her ability to change her behavior quickly. Then I told her I had developed a system to facilitate behavioral change, which you and I will do together in succeeding chapters. First, let's examine the major changes Barbara made.

Core Identity: Balancing her Core Identity, by changing the industry in which she would pursue a new position, made her a bit anxious. Finally, she relaxed and realized that if the balanced Core Identity was not exactly right, she had the tools to re-evaluate herself and change it. Barbara was delighted with her newfound flexibility and told me how relaxed she felt.

The Right Fit: Shaping Her Brand: A friend of Barbara's suggested an opportunity to her that matched her new balanced Core Identity, and she decided to "go for it." Then, based on the information she had, we determined that Barbara matched the employer's blueprint. Barbara was surprised to learn that we would not tailor the Right Fit résumé to match that specific position until she spoke with the employer first. She was also accustomed to sending a cover letter that explained how she fit a particular position, accompanied by a general résumé suitable for all positions. Barbara presumed that a cover letter was a substitute for the Right Fit résumé, and I explained that it was not. No cover letter! And it was too soon to create and send the résumé.

Package to Pitch: Selling Her Brand: I taught Barbara to create a broadcast to demonstrate the exquisite match between her and the employer, one that included a wide array of components to capture the employer's interest over the telephone. Yes, she would make a cold call to verify first whether she was the Right Fit. I carefully coached her on how to make a cold call, a skill I will teach you later in this book. Her first goal was to confirm the fit and then, if she was the Right Fit, to arrange an interview.

Barbara telephoned me after she spoke with the employer. Her voice was steady but filled with excitement. She spoke with real enthusiasm and seemed ready to hit the ground running. I knew that she had succeeded. She had confirmed that she was the Right Fit and had arranged an interview without sending a résumé. Barbara was thrilled that my approach worked. She told me the employer had commented that she was exactly right for the position and wanted to meet with her as soon as possible. Barbara and I then worked together to tailor the résumé to show the Right Fit, incorporating the "matching" information obtained from the phone conversation to further reinforce her fit. She then e-mailed the résumé to the employer before the interview.

Manage the Process: Sharing Her Brand: Before Barbara left for her interview at the Hollywood law firm, I told her to keep reminding herself to Manage the Process and articulate her Right Fit. I made it clear that it was her responsibility to take charge of the interview and say what needed to be said. She was apprehensive because she was accustomed simply to wait for the employer to ask questions to which she would respond. I reminded her that to achieve career success the Right Fit Way, she had to Manage the Process in order to elicit not just an offer, but a very inviting offer. She vowed to shore up her courage and do it.

When Barbara met the law partners, she greeted them with a warm smile and a firm handshake. Immediately, she set the stage for success. Without hesitation, she began managing the process, fending off objections about her youth and lack of experience in entertainment law. Barbara persuaded the partners to craft an offer. She was subtle but effective, relentlessly focusing on the fit.

Following a three-hour interview, one that included a sumptuous lunch of poached salmon at a Hollywood bistro, the partners mentioned that she was the first person they had interviewed, but her pitch had convinced them that they didn't need to interview others. They were ready to proceed with Barbara.

The Calculated Close: Finishing the Deal Before It's Done: For most candidates, including Barbara, discussing compensation is not easy, especially when you fear that asking for too large a salary might jeopardize finalizing the offer. In managing the process, Barbara remembered to gradually insert into the conversation her financial expectations as well as to ask targeted questions to determine whether she could elicit an offer she ultimately would accept. By following my advice and speaking forthrightly, Barbara finished the deal quite comfortably and without irritating the partners. She was ready to execute her new balanced Core Identity as an entertainment lawyer.

The Total Package: The Flawless Fit: To be sure every aspect of the fit was exactly right, Barbara had to make changes to her hair, makeup, clothes, stockings, shoes, jewelry, handbag, and briefcase. Before she did, she studied the "look" of entertainment lawyers, finagling an invitation to an event at which she could study them in their native habitat. Together, she and I created the plan for her makeover, which included coloring her prematurely gray hair and restyling it. After she spent several hours in a salon, Barbara's highlighted, honey-blonde hair now framed her heart-shaped face. She then proceeded to implement the rest of our makeover to prepare for the interview.

In Barbara's case we didn't need to focus on other elements of the Total Package because she truly was "the total package." She was "the right fit," setting a standard against which no one else could compete. The makeover was simply the final touch to ensure that the partners would offer her the position because she met and exceeded their expectations. After Barbara signed her offer, we met for lunch. She was thrilled with her success, understanding now how to Win Without Competing, and delighted to forget the competition. I reminded her to continue to Manage the Process in her new position to ensure long-term success.

Trigger Tip
Win Without Competing against others

Let's go!

CHAPTER TWO

Make No Assumptions: Open Those Doors

Your Goal:
Recognize the negative consequences of making assumptions and stop making them.

THIS IS THE BEST advice I or anyone can offer you: Don't make assumptions—not ever—not about your career goals and objectives, and not about anything else in your life. As author Erica Jong observed, we make our own prisons. I'm convinced we build them chiefly out of the assumptions we make, assumptions that almost always impede our progress toward the most favorable outcomes in our lives.

During the time I headed a $60-million education program for the National Cancer Institute at the National Institutes of Health, my colleagues and I hoped to enlist the assistance of renowned medical researcher Jonas Salk, who had developed the polio vaccine in 1954 and saved hundreds of thousands of people from this crippling disease. The medical

25

oncologists with whom I worked had mailed several letters to Dr. Salk at the Salk Institute in La Jolla, California, requesting an initial meeting, but they hadn't yet received a reply. While I was attending a professional meeting in nearby San Diego, I decided to attempt a different strategy. Although I understood that directly telephoning his office to ask for an appointment was perhaps a bit forward, it also certainly seemed worth the risk—I couldn't fail to reach Dr. Salk any more completely than my colleagues already had, after all. And because I refused to assume that I *couldn't* make an appointment with Jonas Salk by phone, I tried—and I succeeded. Dr. Salk's assistant kindly listened to my request, then scheduled an appointment. A few days later, Dr. Salk graciously met with me for more than an hour.

At one point during our time together, Dr. Salk suddenly and without a word of explanation left the room. Was the meeting over? Should I leave? I wondered. But I opted instead to make *no assumptions* about what his disappearance meant and simply waited to see what would happen next. After several minutes, he returned with a number of documents cradled in his arm, publications authored by him that he hoped would assist and encourage us in our research program. As I departed, he escorted me to the door and blew me a kiss goodbye. How charming he was! Back in Washington, my colleagues were astounded by my chutzpah and delighted by my success—an outcome I simply never assumed I couldn't accomplish.

Let me introduce a candidate I'll call Colin, a remarkable man whom I recently had the pleasure to assist in finding and securing a position for which he is very well qualified, one in which his talents are enormously appreciated by his prestigious employer, and the kind of mid-career advancement that offers him both satisfaction and security—a Right Fit for

Colin and his new employer in every way.

Colin, in his early forties, is a native of Ireland; he was lured to the United States fifteen years ago by one of the country's leading cancer-research hospitals to direct its clinical information systems. During that decade and a half, he developed a well-deserved reputation as one of the world's leaders in a field that applies advanced information technology to cutting-edge medical research. Colin's colleagues praised his myriad skills and loved working alongside him; he remained happy in his position. However, he was increasingly aware that he had accomplished the goals he had set for himself there, and he ultimately determined it was time for a new challenge in a new city, in a place where he and his family could create the kind of home they had dreamed of for so long. Canada appealed to them. They loved the countryside and were eager to escape from a large metropolis where they couldn't afford to buy a home.

When Colin discovered that a Canadian research hospital—one with an international reputation comparable to that of his current employer—had begun to advertise for a new director of clinical information systems, he was intrigued, then excited, then quickly disappointed. The published position description stated that the employer was interested only in candidates who possessed advanced degrees, preferably a PhD, while Colin had risen to the top of his field with only a BA. When he and I first spoke, Colin remained interested in the position, but he didn't think he should bother to apply. He could read, after all, and the employer wanted to hire someone with a PhD. I assured Colin that I could read as well, but I also explained that if we were to work together successfully, he would have to adopt and take completely to heart the first rule of my Right Fit Method: *Don't make assumptions*.

Certainly, Colin and the position that intrigued him would have to prove to be the Right Fit. We wouldn't know whether they were until we had created a comprehensive blueprint for the position and compared Colin's collective skills, training, and experience to it. But what we *wouldn't* do as we began the blueprint process was assume that Colin was the wrong fit simply because he lacked one of the qualifications the employer deemed important. This was a career door Colin couldn't possibly open if he assumed from the outset that it was a door he wouldn't be permitted to walk through. We had just begun determining whether Colin was well matched to this particular position—and we were oceans away from winning him an interview or an offer—but before we could begin the journey, it was essential that Colin not paralyze himself or the process with too-early estimations about what was possible and what was not.

During the course of my search and placement career, I've discovered that candidates for professional positions commonly make five assumptions that lead to detrimental, if not disastrous, career decisions, assumptions that limit their vision and ultimately prevent them from fulfilling their dreams. As I've already made clear, *any* assumption is a perilous one, but these five are particularly dangerous. Sadly, I find that people make these assumptions over and over again.

1. *Employees assume that, if given the option by their employer, it's wiser for them to accept downsizing—in other words, no job at all—than to accept a lesser position within the company.*

But actually: Accepting downsizing is your *last* alternative, not your first, unless you're a CEO or a very high-level corporate executive. And even at the top rungs of the ladder, it's often better to use some ingenuity to restructure your role in the company rather than find yourself out on the street. Remember, future employers aren't going to view you as "downsized" or "in transition." To them, you are simply unemployed. When you are employed, you operate from strength and can negotiate your options accordingly. But when you're unemployed, your strengths are stripped away, and whether you deserve it or not, you look far too much like a failure for comfort. It isn't fair, but it's true.

2. People searching for employment, regardless of their current employment status, assume that search firms are quite careful about protecting their confidentiality.

But actually: When you give a search firm your résumé, it's critically important for you to find out what that firm plans to do with it. In certain parts of the country, it's common practice for search firms to broadcast, via e-mail or fax, their candidates' résumés to companies and organizations. But if you or another search firm happens to contact those same employers, their response—count on it—will be "no interest." The search firm is neither your mother nor your father, and ultimately only you can protect yourself. Remember, your résumé is a precious illustration of your background, experience, and accomplishments. You *must* maintain its value, value that's lost forever when it becomes nothing more than a search firm's unwelcome spam. And if your résumé is reduced to spam, who will view *you* as anything other than spam?

3. Candidates assume that by the time an open position is posted, companies and organizations have a clear and well-defined understanding of the opening they seek to fill.

But actually: Clearly defining a position and who is right for it takes time and creativity. Far too often, employers have only the dimmest sense of the parameters of a position they seek to fill or the kind of candidate they believe will be the Right Fit for the situation. In fact, that's often the fundamental reason why they choose to examine—and even interview—a long parade of candidates; it's only as the parade passes by that they clarify for themselves what the position will entail and what kind of person can best fill it.

4. *Individuals in search of a perfect opportunity assume their odds of finding it are greatly improved when they broadcast their résumés as widely as they can, which, in this remarkable information age, means all around the globe.*

But actually: Broadcasting your desire to change positions is unwise for several reasons. If your employer learns of your actions, he or she may well summarily determine that you're disloyal and either reprimand you or ultimately send you packing. If you use company e-mail to broadcast your résumé, you can be fired on the spot. And perhaps most fundamentally, remember that if you broadcast your availability from Burbank to Bombay, you'll appear desperate or mediocre or desperately mediocre, and who will want to hire you in that case? Employers like to believe in every instance that they've captured the very top talent. But are the most talented people out there really sending their résumés out so widely and distantly that they seem to be searching for life on other planets?

5. *People who have set their sights on a particular position assume it's not appropriate to telephone company management to discuss the opening and their active interest in it.*

But actually: Calling high-level management personnel without an appointment can, in point of fact, be very effective and may well be the only way you can reach them, interact with them, and influence them to your benefit. Try calling early in the day or late in the day to catch them personally, instead of their assistants. If you know how to frame your call and what to say, briefly, you just might speak with a decision maker who'll agree to meet with you in person to discuss an open position—long before your interview. I'll address this often-valuable opportunity later in the book. Remember that I successfully arranged a meeting with the legendary Jonas Salk simply by calling and proposing one. You can do it, too!

Faulty Assumptions Employers Often Make

The research hospital struggled, without success, for nearly a year to find the "best" person for the clinical informations system position, which Colin wanted with all his heart. Richard Jameson, who headed the hospital's human resources department, had advertised widely, attracted great interest in the position, and by now had read hundreds of résumés, conducted dozens of telephone interviews, and invited numerous candidates to interview in person, all without success. It was critical to get this vitally important position filled as soon as possible, yet somehow, every time she, Jenna Phillips—the hospital's vice president for clinical research—and other key staff anxiously examined the leading candidates, the "best" of the large group either had just accepted a position elsewhere, was no longer interested, or failed to impress in a second interview.

In determining the necessary qualifications for the position, Richard and Jenna had made a costly assumption—one that had kept many potentially compelling candidates at bay. Someone capable of leading the institution's cutting-edge clinical information-systems program necessarily would have an impressive academic background, they had assumed. Yet both professionals failed to consider that the IT world has evolved so dramatically over the past twenty years that its best and brightest new talent emerged not from

(continued on pp. 32 and 33)

(continued from p. 31)

long-established university programs but rather from tiny entrepreneurial start-ups with curious names like Oracle, Yahoo!, Google, and a hundred others. Many of the finest information-systems experts in the United States didn't have bachelor's degrees, let alone PhDs, and the assumption that the "best" candidate for the hospital's position would have wallpapered his office with degrees was entirely at odds with industry realities.

*A*ssumptions employers make are every bit as detrimental to finding the Right Fit as the counterproductive assumptions of candidates. Thousands of managers like Richard and Jenna mistakenly assume that they should search the world for the "best" candidate. They assume that a search for the best will consume at least half a year, even a whole year; finding the best can be a lot like searching for a peanut in a super-sized tub of popcorn, Richard liked to say. Managers who make his mistake assume a generalized, boilerplate position description is all they need to envision, produce, and post in order for hundreds of stellar résumés to begin showing up in the in-boxes.

Yet each of those assumptions is mistaken; each works *against* a successful hire, rather than for it. In reality, companies and organizations who don't carefully analyze their needs *before* they post a position opening, creating a position-specific blueprint of their needs and the specs of the candidate they desire, are crippling the process from the outset. And those who believe it's best to leave the position description vague so they can mold it to a spectacular candidate are limiting their organization's vision and risking the hiring of a very wrong fit, albeit someone with eye-catching credentials. And by taking months and months to watch a battalion of candidates march by, trying to decide who is "best," they squander time and human resources that could have been far better spent determining in detail what the company's true needs are and the ideal candidate to meet them.

Without the implementation of the Right Fit Method, absent a shift of the process from searching for the "best" candidate to carefully evaluating their hospital's true needs, Richard and Jenna never would have given Colin—whom everyone on the hospital's clinical research team is now thrilled to have among them—a second look, not because he didn't deserve one, but because their series of ruinous assumptions were leading their search far away from the Right Fit.

What assumptions do you make?

Let's find out. You're working. It's lunchtime and you need a break. You decide that instead of going out, you will stay at your desk and play on your computer.

Next to each statement, check TRUE or FALSE. I can:

	TRUE	FALSE
■ Send personal e-mails.	_____	_____
■ Read personal e-mails.	_____	_____
■ Play solitaire.	_____	_____
■ Delete e-mails that I don't want anyone to read.	_____	_____
■ Search Monster and other websites to look for a new opportunity.	_____	_____
■ Send my résumé to other employers.	_____	_____
■ Shop for food.	_____	_____
■ Buy my vacation airline tickets.	_____	_____
■ Send jokes to my friends.	_____	_____
■ Do what I want with my e-mail during lunch.	_____	_____

What assumptions did *you* make?

Let's find out. Record your Assumptions Quotient (AQ) here: _____

Marked all 10 questions false. You did it!	100%
Marked 6 questions false. Walking on eggshells.	60%
Marked 0 questions false. Leave before you are fired.	0%

 ## Employer Management of Employee E-mail and Internet

Let's set the record straight. No one is above firing! Many companies require new employees to sign a document that delineates the proper and improper use of their terminals. If you are asked to sign such a document, it is highly likely that people have been hired to observe your behavior on the computer. I'm amazed when I speak to employee groups that almost everyone assumes that work computers can be used for personal needs. They also assume that if the e-mails are deleted, they are gone. Be careful. Although they appear to be deleted, those messages remain on the company's server. Your employer can view your deleted e-mails, even months after you sent them. The bottom line is that you cannot assume that you have any privacy on your office computer.

Remember your AQ!
If you scored below 100 percent,
you are in a danger zone at work.
Make no more assumptions.

In order to use my Right Fit Method, it is crucial that you learn to speak up to get what you want and need. To do this, you cannot make any assumptions about what is possible and not possible. To illustrate this point, let me relate one of my favorite stories, one I call "The Airline Produced a Plane."

I was traveling from New York City to Toledo, Ohio, on a business trip. It was snowing. I missed my connecting flight. No problem, I thought. I'll simply ask the airline for another plane. I asked, and, sure enough, the airline produced a plane! To be honest, it was a small plane, but my fellow passengers and I were delighted, and I arrived on time for my meeting. If I had assumed that procuring a second plane was impossible, I would have spent the whole night in the airport and missed my morning meeting.

Why do we make assumptions? It's an automatic response. You've trained yourself to do so. But now, I want you to practice *not* making assumptions. To do this, you need to become aware how frequently you make assumptions, and then stop making them.

After you read the example below, turn to your Activities Journal on page 37 and record *one* assumption a day for seven days that led you to behave inappropriately and resulted in negative consequences. Next to it, record the inappropriate behavior and its consequences. Select your assumptions from your personal or professional life or both.

Here's an example of an assumption gone terribly awry: After an interview, a candidate for a new position assumed that the employer was not interested in her because many months elapsed and the employer communicated nothing. She ultimately accepted another position that she did not particularly want, only to find out later that the first opportunity, which was highly desirable, was not "dead." After five months, the "dead" employer called with an attractive offer, but the candidate believed she shouldn't abandon her new employer, so she lost a very desirable position because of her original—and erroneous—assumption.

At this time, I want you to learn how to stop making automatic assumptions.

Week 1

For a week, keep a diary of an assumption you make each day and the inappropriate behavior and consequences it spawns.

Week 2

Record nothing.

Week 3

Repeat Week 1, if you haven't kicked the assumption habit yet. As you kick the habit, your stress level will go down. I promise.

As an aid to help you remember not to make automatic assumptions, remember this:

Trigger Tip
The Airline Produced a Plane

Let's fly!

ACTIVITIES JOURNAL	
Week 1	
Record an assumption a day.	**Record the inappropriate behavior.**
	Record the negative consequences.
Monday	
Tuesday	
Wednesday	
Thursday	
Friday	
Saturday	
Sunday	

ACTIVITIES JOURNAL

Week 3 (Remember, you do not record Week 2.)

Record an assumption a day.	Record the inappropriate behavior.
	Record the negative consequences.
Monday	
Tuesday	
Wednesday	
Thursday	
Friday	
Saturday	
Sunday	

CHAPTER THREE

Cereal, Eggs, or Yogurt: The Small Changes Come First

Your Goal:
Make small changes in your personal and professional daily routines that set the stage for bigger changes.

STUCK IN A RUT? Tired of not achieving what you strive for? Are you doing the same things over and over again and wondering why you don't get the results you want? Well, if so, at least you're not alone. Over the years, I've had dozens of candidates who have despaired of ever reaching their career goals. On the other hand, I've had almost as many who have powerfully achieved their career goals—and so can you. Let me share the story of one of them—a remarkable woman I'll call Laurie—and show you how she ultimately seized the success she always hoped could be hers.

39

Laurie called me two years after she had heard me speak at a professional meeting. "You were radically different from my traditional headhunter colleagues," she explained during our first phone conversation. "You were organized and had an approach that was different and proactive, rather than just letting someone's résumé sit in a filing drawer somewhere. You told the meeting audience that the *candidate* needed to take charge, and I remember being fascinated." Then she added, "Back then, I wasn't really happy with my job, but I wasn't ready to do something aggressive about finding a great one."

By now, however, Laurie wanted to get focused and to make some lasting changes in her life because her situation had grown urgent. "I know I've got to find a new job, the perfect job for me, and I need to find it now. I'm not getting anywhere on my own, and I feel a little desperate. My son is about to enter high school. If I don't act now, I'll have to wait another four years to make a change, and I can't bear the thought of waiting that long. If I do, I'll go out of my mind."

Laurie explained to me that the stress of maintaining her current career as a professor and educational consultant had begun to take a great toll, even on her health. "I'm swallowing Maalox like it's candy. My hair is falling out. I'm not sleeping. I've lost weight I didn't need to lose. I'm a wreck."

As Laurie spoke, I could see what a precarious situation she was in. But why did she wait two years to act, allowing her health to suffer so significantly in the process? I learned during that first conversation that Laurie holds a doctoral degree—from *Columbia*—but everything she told me made it appear that she was behaving in ways that didn't reflect the intelligent and very capable person she obviously was. While I listened, it became clear to me that Laurie was repeating the same ineffective behaviors she had repeated for years but was naively expecting a different outcome each time. She knew she needed to effect a massive change in her career, but she wasn't doing anything new—let alone anything proven and effective—in order to achieve it.

Before we ended that first conversation, I was able to get Laurie's assurance that she would dedicate herself to making some profound changes in her life—including several that would not be easy—and to assure her that with her strong resolve and commitment, I could help her.

My similar goal is to help *you* change your behaviors in ways that will enable you to take control of your life and find the position that's the Right Fit for you, and to do so long before you become sick and desperate like Laurie. The alternative, if you burn out and give up, could be a disaster.

I'm happy to report that Laurie's story does have a wonderful ending, and I'll describe her remarkable transformation on subsequent pages. I want your career story to have a happy ending as well. Use a task-driven approach to change, rather than a scattered, whimsical one. Remember, *the small changes come first.* Once you've demonstrated to yourself that you can accomplish the small changes, the bigger changes don't seem nearly so daunting.

In the introduction, I mentioned that together we would undertake a number of activities, tasks that will specifically help you achieve the objectives detailed in each chapter of *Win Without Competing!* As you move through the book, you'll successfully complete each of these tasks. As of this moment, *you are in training.* And we're preparing you to Win Without Competing—our ultimate goal.

To record your activities, proceed to your Activities Journal on page 46 of this chapter. Record each of your activities there, and be sure to reward yourself for successfully completing each activity. (I'll leave the reward to you.) Let's begin.

I believe we *should* sweat the small stuff. Paying attention to every detail enables us to do even bigger things in our lives. So, let's get started by changing the way you eat breakfast. It's a small thing, yes, but a very important one. If you don't currently eat breakfast, or you do so only sporadically, this is an opportunity to improve your health as well as prove to yourself that you *can* make lasting changes in your life.

Week 1

For a week, keep a diary of what you eat for breakfast in your *Win Without Competing!* journal. And if you find yourself saying, "I don't need to do this because I eat the same thing every single day," that's an erroneous assumption. Keep the record!

Review your diary after your seventh breakfast. What did you learn? Are you eating the same breakfast or changing daily? Let's shake things up!

Now create a breakfast menu for all of Week 2 and record the menu in your journal. You will be planning seven new breakfasts, and because I like to eat healthy, may I make a few recommendations?

What about wild salmon (smoked, baked, or broiled); fresh blueberries, raspberries, or strawberries with yogurt? Check out goat's-milk yogurt, if you haven't tried it. It's wonderful. Try French toast made with egg whites. Scrambled egg whites with Roma tomatoes, onions, and peppers, and add some smoked wild salmon if you'd like. Organic hot cereals are great: buckwheat, oatmeal, white-corn grits, and barley. Try adding some small pieces of crystallized ginger. It's delicious. Eating a healthy, varied, and tasty breakfast can bring a lot that's good to your life. (And by the way, I'm always looking for new breakfast ideas. Please e-mail me at drbarro@winwithoutcompeting.com with your healthy suggestions.) Bon appétit!

Week 2

After you've eaten your seventh breakfast of Week 2, create another seven-day breakfast menu and record it under Week 3 in your journal. This time, you can repeat one breakfast from the second week's menu or change daily. Be sure to record in your Activities Journal whether you ate the breakfasts you planned.

Week 3

Enjoy your breakfasts during this third week. Be sure to record in your Activities Journal whether you ate the breakfasts you planned.

Week 4

Eat precisely what you want for breakfast and record daily what you have eaten. At the end of Week 4, it's time to evaluate not only what you've consumed for breakfast but your behavioral changes as well. What did you eat during Week 4?

Did you have a different breakfast every day? Or four different breakfasts and three that were the same? If, during Week 4, you ate the same breakfast every day, I'm sorry, but you're going to have to repeat this activity. But if you had a different breakfast every day, your behavioral change was remarkably successful, and you've proven to yourself that you're capable of making significant and lasting change. That's the ideal, of course. Strive to achieve this goal. It's only breakfast, yes, but you need to learn how to change your behavior quickly to excel at implementing my Right Fit Method.

What did you eat in Week 4?

_____

Evaluate your behavioral change. Record your change
quotient (CQ) here _____

Ate a different breakfast daily.	You did it!	100%
Ate 4 different breakfasts, 3 the same.	Slipping back?	60%
Ate the same breakfast daily.	Repeat the 4-week plan	0%

Next, practice making more small modifications in your
daily routine that will help you learn both the challenges—
and the rewards—of behavioral change. For example, drive to
work using a new route. If you work at home, get dressed, take
a brisk walk, then return home and dive into your work. The
goal is to become more and more flexible in the ways in which
you alter your behavior. Even though I've learned how to
change my behavior very quickly to achieve my objectives, I
continue practicing every day. *Rigidity is the enemy of creativity,* I discovered long ago.

And now, it's time to begin making small changes in your
professional life.

Begin by changing the order in which you perform daily
tasks in your office. For example, if you always look at your
e-mail in-box first, change that behavior and begin checking
your voice-mail first.

As a bigger challenge, I want you to begin the day doing
something you plainly do not like to do. For example, if you
hate making marketing calls, hop to it and do this first. And
record in your journal how many days you needed to implement each of these two changes in your routine.

If you needed several days, I have to be frank and tell you that's not good. You must train yourself to change quickly. If you are still doing nothing more than thinking about making changes, it's time to carefully examine why you are stalling or blocked and what you can do to free yourself to change. I don't want to leave you behind.

If, on the other hand, you implemented the two new changes in your office routine immediately, congratulations. You're ready to embark on the road to success you have been dreaming about. I am preparing you to become a career-strategy expert. To do this, I'll introduce you to other changes you'll need to make. For now, just remember this Trigger Tip and use it to reinforce the behaviors you have changed.

Trigger Tip
Rigidity is the enemy of creativity

Time is marching on—away we go!

ACTIVITIES JOURNAL

Week 1
Record what you eat for breakfast.
Monday
Tuesday
Wednesday
Thursday
Friday
Saturday
Sunday

ACTIVITIES JOURNAL

Week 2	Week 3
Record your seven-day menu.	**Record your seven-day menu.**
Each day, mark a plus (+) if you ate the breakfast you planned, or a minus (-) if you did not.	**Each day, mark a plus (+) if you ate the breakfast you planned, or a minus (-) if you did not.**
Monday (+) or (-) ☐	Monday (+) or (-) ☐
Tuesday (+) or (-) ☐	Tuesday (+) or (-) ☐
Wednesday (+) or (-) ☐	Wednesday (+) or (-) ☐
Thursday (+) or (-) ☐	Thursday (+) or (-) ☐
Friday (+) or (-) ☐	Friday (+) or (-) ☐
Saturday (+) or (-) ☐	Saturday (+) or (-) ☐
Sunday (+) or (-) ☐	Sunday (+) or (-) ☐

I hope you had all plusses!

ACTIVITIES JOURNAL

Week 4
Record what you eat for breakfast.
Monday
Tuesday
Wednesday
Thursday
Friday
Saturday
Sunday

ORDER OF DAILY OFFICE TASKS

How many days did it take to implement each change?

If you had any difficulty implementing either change, record the reasons why and try again.

Don't give up. Take it step-by-step. You can do it!

ACT II

How the Right Fit Method Works

CHAPTER FOUR

Your Core Identity:
Know Thyself Now

Your Goal:
Create a balanced
core identity.

Laying the Foundation

THE FORTY-YEAR CAREER in the same organization is becoming extinct. Mergers and acquisitions that lead to
downsizing have forced huge numbers of employees out of
their positions. Many must change careers because they cannot find similar positions. Some, nervous about the sudden
downsizing, accept the first position offered to them, even
though it may not be the Right Fit. Others remain unemployed
for long periods. But out of the chaos, some seize the opportunity to re-think who they are and what they want to do, forging
new career identities that ultimately lead to great success.

Unhappy employees abound in the workplace for a variety of reasons. Fear of downsizing is common, but there's more

51

to the story. Employees constantly tell me that their current positions are the wrong fit for them. In varying states of frenzy, some of them become so frustrated and furious that they vow to make significant changes. But many make the wrong choices. From extensive interviews, I've learned that a serious part of the problem for many employees is that they fail to Manage the Process at work, something that often can eliminate or alleviate their unhappiness. The bottom line is that you must always try to improve your current situation before you take other steps—unless it's simply impossible to do so. Finding a new opportunity, especially if you are unemployed, is not a simple matter.

Remember Laurie? When she called to ask me to coach her, she wanted to leave her university position, one she was convinced could not be fixed. Her professional situation and her poor health demanded that she change positions as soon as possible—Laurie was dangerously out of balance. As we determined her Core Identity, I was able to convince her that it would be difficult for me to coach her to stardom—the deanship of a school—if she were unemployed. She agreed not to leave her position prematurely and to Manage the Process both at work and at home until we achieved her goal.

A word of caution. Changing Core Identities is an absolute necessity for some. However, too often people change their Core Identities hoping that the identity will be a panacea or a solution to long-term inner unhappiness. In talking with hundreds of candidates and employees and reviewing their résumés, I've learned how common it is for individuals to invest significant time and money in professional development, only to discover they don't like the careers they've newly trained for. I once met, for example, a board-certified pathologist who decided his current career was not right for him. So he went back to school, studying to become an orthopedic surgeon. But he wasn't happy with that choice either, and he became editor-in-chief of a health publication that failed. Next, he decided to study gemology. Ultimately, he became a gemologist who sold jewelry and a freelance writer specializing in medical subjects.

Switching careers is *not* the solution to inner unhappiness. If you're discontented, figure out what's really eating at you and confront it. Please be very sure that if you decide to change your Core Identity, you do so because it is the Right Fit for you and that your gut agrees. Multiple Core Identities over a lifetime must make sense and enable you to achieve career objectives that meet both personal and professional needs. Otherwise, you'll never have inner peace.

The National Society of Hispanic MBAs (NSHMBA) invited me to conduct a workshop on the Right Fit Method. Grace Tiscareno-Sato, a member of NSHMBA, interviewed me for the organization's national newsletter.

During our interview, I learned that Grace was currently the global marketing manager of Unified Communications at Siemens Communications, a company that has about 50,000 employees globally, but she added that she had come to that position by way of a dramatic career change. I was eager to learn more about Grace and invited her to become a storyteller.

When Grace's story arrived in my e-mail in-box, I read it quickly and immediately called her to find out more. I think you'll find her story fascinating. She is the oldest of five children. Her father was a tailor and her mother became a seamstress in mid-career, after many years as a homemaker. When Grace was fourteen, her ninth-grade drafting instructor encouraged her to become an architect, and she became intrigued by a career that would allow her to pursue both her technical and creative capabilities.

During her senior year in high school, Grace applied to the University of California at Berkeley, the number one architectural school in the country; concurrently, she applied for an Air Force ROTC (Reserve Officer Training Corp) scholarship. On the same day, Grace received both her letter of acceptance to Berkeley and notification of her ROTC scholarship, one that would lead to her commission as an Air Force officer when she graduated.

Now, I want to invite Grace onstage to give us a glimpse, in her own words, of her journey from architecture to military aviation to global marketing and communications.

After a ten-year military aviation career, I knew it was time for a change. I had logged thousands of flying hours as a senior crewmember and flight instructor on military refueling jets and had visited dozens of nations. I had also completed my thesis for my master's degree in international business management with an emphasis in global marketing while working in a non-flying staff position at the U.S. embassy in Quito, Ecuador.

At this point, I was feeling confident that I wanted to pursue global marketing as a career. Why? From my military experience, I learned that I loved working in the international arena. As a teenager, I had experienced the pleasure of writing articles and creating content—critical marketing skills. In college, I was elected PR director for the Cal Marching Band. And while in Italy, I became fascinated with mobile technologies. I put these passions and skills together and knew global marketing and communications was the right career direction for me.

In addition, I was no longer happy to just keep flying to the same countries every year, as well as being away from my husband for months at a time, and I really felt the need to apply my newly found knowledge in the private sector. So the day I presented my thesis, I put in my paperwork to separate from the military.

My plan was to get through the six-month separation process, take six months off to enjoy downhill skiing as much as possible, meditate on what exactly I wanted to do next, then begin the process of interviewing for a new position. Fortunately, I had been actively networking with the civilian community outside the base for years, had been extremely active as part of a nonprofit organization, and had kept in touch with colleagues who had left the Air Force ahead of me and found employment in the local community. I had also been brought into a very special group of women who met monthly to move each others' lives forward in whatever way they could. Each member of this small group of local professional women—artists, small-business owners, and educators—was hand-picked by its founder, Julia Hubbel, for the simple reason that Julia knew each person had something to give to the group.

What happened was that the week after I separated, I was surfing the web and came across an organization called the National Society of Hispanic MBAs (NSHMBA). They were hosting a national career conference in Denver and their website said that over four hundred companies would be present in a huge career fair specifically recruiting candidates of Hispanic descent. So, although I had promised myself some well-earned decompression time, there I was on an airplane to Denver, newly crafted résumé in my portfolio, ready to begin the process of interviewing for my next career.

Within six weeks of attending the conference, I had flown to second- and third-round interviews with a major defense contractor that really wanted to hire me into supply chain management work in Phoenix, Arizona. I had a generous offer on the table that included a $40,000 signing bonus and a complete relocation package. At the same time, I had been conducting informational interviews with those in the Hubbel Group and with people from their personal networks. I had repeatedly expressed in our meetings that I was passionate about global marketing and that I was passionate about the communications industry. I had met several people that had provided the insight I needed into what was involved in this new function and new industry, neither of which I had any experience in whatsoever, although my graduate studies had delved deeply into both. I had been told that the first thing I needed to do was a thorough self-assessment. I was told, "You have so much potential, so much energy, so much intelligence, but you have absolutely no idea how or where to focus it right now. You need first to understand your passions and interests before you seriously start looking for a new position." They were so right. I did an excellent self-assessment with one of the members who was a professional career coach and learned exactly what I wanted to do and the kind of environment I wanted to work in.

So imagine the group's surprise when one day I announced that I had a job offer in Phoenix with a defense contractor! The questions were pointed: Why would you even consider such a thing? What does this have to do with your passion for marketing and for communications? If you accept this job, who will you know in the communications industry in five years? I realized I had made a grave error. I had let myself be lured into an obvious choice for a military flight instructor/aircrew member; the lucrative business of defense contracting is one that draws many former military officers. I had wanted to find out what I'd be worth to that industry, and now I knew it was a lot. But the voices of the Hubbel Group were my saviors. They were there to remind me to follow *my* passion, to do the work I *loved* to do, and not be swayed by the opinions and interests of others.

So, I did the unthinkable for someone in my position at the time. I declined the job offer with the fat signing bonus, knowing that it would lead nowhere I wanted to go. Yes, it would put money in my pocket, but wouldn't be true to what I wanted. It was such an incredibly easy decision to make, and I felt so empowered doing it. I was looking this offer in the face and saying, it's not good enough. It's just money. That I had the guts to do that still amazes me seven years later.

Four months after leaving the Air Force, I hooked up with a recruiting agency that specialized in placing junior military officers in corporate America. I enjoyed the winter, skied a lot, kept meeting with the Hubbel Group, kept learning via informational interviews, attended some job conferences, and continued to fly to the San Francisco Bay Area for interviews. I got two other offers in other industries, which I also declined. I was building up my confidence to be able to interview with anyone, anywhere. I was paving the way for my dream job that I just *knew* was out there, and I knew I'd be very ready to secure it when it made itself known.

Next, I did something very smart—I tapped into my personal network in the Bay Area. I had graduated from UC Berkeley, and most of my friends from the Cal Marching Band, Air Force ROTC, and architecture school were in the Bay Area. So, I composed a quick note telling them exactly what I was searching for and asked for their help in finding this position I knew had to exist somewhere. Within thirty minutes of sending that e-mail, I received a response from a friend who was a hiring manager for a European communications company. She wrote, "You won't believe this but I just finished writing a job description for a position I'm about to begin interviewing for, that matches exactly what you're looking for. Take a look." She attached the description and when I opened it, I couldn't believe my eyes. There it was: Global Marketing Manager, Unified Messaging Applications, the functional role I was seeking at one of the world's largest communications companies!

I flew down and interviewed first with my friend, a person who had seen me in action during our college days when I was the spokesperson and public relations director for the university's marching band. I ultimately interviewed with five of her colleagues as well, and they unanimously nominated me as their top candidate. I relocated to Northern California in late spring and began work at my dream job seven months after leaving the military. The women of the Hubbel Group threw me a going-away party, and I was so grateful to them all for their invaluable guidance. Six years later, I'm still happy in the communications industry, having added more and more responsibility each year that I've spent with my employer.

Let's examine the reasons behind the decisions Grace made, and how she felt about her choices as she changed her Core Identity and rebalanced herself. Grace always moved toward her goal and never ran away from anything. Her approach was thoughtful, logical, and systematic. Her insight into her needs enabled her to balance and rebalance.

Why did Grace initially select architecture?

In high school, she analyzed her capabilities and how she wanted to use them, and with the advice of a mentor, she selected architecture:

My AFROTC scholarship was awarded to me to study architecture, which is what I did and ultimately majored in. The Air Force figured I'd study for four years, and then serve four years in a civil-engineering squadron somewhere and that would be that.

Why did Grace become a military aviator?

Halfway through my studies at Cal, I attended the AFROTC Field Training Program (FTP), a four-week leadership training "boot camp" for officer candidates. At this FTP, I had the opportunity to take an orientation flight in a T-37 jet, a small two-seat aerobatic trainer. My instructor pilot was a lady, and I had the best time flying the jet with her. We did rolls, loops, barrel rolls, and all kinds of tricks for a full hour over the Arizona desert. I was hooked!

At the end of FTP, you get rated/scored on your physical fitness performance, leadership skills, academic skills, etc. Once you return to your training unit, the staff meets with you to tell you how you did. In my case, I had kicked butt, and the staff encouraged me to apply for an aviation "slot," decided by a national board of officers that reviews training records and staff recommendations.

I figured, "why not?" What a great opportunity to be offered. I figured if I could get one of the handful of flight-training positions available (especially the very few allocated to women), I would fly right after college and do architecture and civil engineering later in my life. So, I put my name in the hat and a few months later, the board of officers chose me to attend military flight training. Realizing I had been one of only twenty-nine women chosen nationwide to attend flight training that year, I immediately jumped on the chance and accepted the appointment.

In short, I had prepared myself for other opportunities to come along and when an amazing one did, I seized it. Having a technical class-load, doing well academically at a highly respected, highly competitive school like Berkeley (and at FTP academics), and having the highest scores in physical fitness all came together. My reward was this incredible opportunity to go fly for the Air Force.

Why did Grace leave the military and her position?

She decided the fit was wrong and could not be fixed. When I interviewed her, I learned that initially she had been very frustrated when she could not fix the fit. Then, she decided to approach her situation strategically rather than emotionally. She resigned from the military when she was ready to implement her plan.

Why did Grace select global marketing and communications?

As she described, Grace was passionate about global marketing and communications, coupled with the fact that she had the right technical and interpersonal skills.

Throughout the changing of Grace's Core Identities, she continued to focus on her clear and focused image of her Right Fit. When she determined that the current fit was no longer right, she made a change that matched her Right Fit standard. She left military aviation to follow her passion for global marketing and communications. She turned down a handsome offer in supply-chain management and others because they, too, were the wrong fit. Her unwavering commitment to identifying and selecting the Right Fit has been the hallmark of her career success.

Grace's professional career is based on her solid, insightful, and deep understanding of who she is and what she wants. Underlying her logical approach is a deep passion, which motivates her career choices and empowers her to succeed and soar to new heights. It is absolutely essential for you to determine, as Grace did, what turns you on. To truly achieve success, you need to follow your passion. To be creative, you need to feel passion. If you work only to achieve money and have no passion, you will feel empty and unfulfilled.

Finding Your Core Identity

The major reason individuals have difficulty determining their Core Identity is that they don't understand how to approach the decision-making process. Almost all of us require a systematic approach to selecting a career. On the surface, it sounds simple, but it's not. We frequently forget that many decisions need to be made in determining our Right Fit careers. For example, if you decide to be a graphic designer or website developer, in what part of the country do you want to live and work? Should you work for someone else or yourself? If you decide to work for someone else, what size company is the Right Fit for you? Do you want to be one of 50,000 employees, one of five, or somewhere in between? Company size has a significant impact on how you function, and underestimating its importance can lead directly to making the wrong choices. If you decide to take the entrepreneurial path, should you work alone or hire employees or independent contractors? Some people believe that they can work alone, only to find out later that they cannot adjust to the solitude. They miss interacting with colleagues and return to a corporate environment.

Do you ever say to yourself, "Wouldn't it be wonderful to figure things out first, before I make the wrong career decisions?" That's precisely what I'm going to show you how to do. My Right Fit Method guides you toward making the right decisions, which will save you time, money, and, very importantly, pain.

To be honest, I hadn't really thought much about pain until Bob Cowan, who in 1966 co-founded the executive-search firm Search West, said as he began to train me, "Arlene, you're looking for the pain." The intensity in his voice stunned me. I couldn't believe that I had selected a new career that required me to focus on pain. Undaunted, I followed his advice. Every time I spoke with a candidate, employee, or employer, I asked questions to elicit pain. I quickly realized that Bob was correct. The vast majority of people with whom I spoke were in some type of pain. And change was very often the instigator of their pain.

Reducing, alleviating, and preventing pain is achievable. The right Core Identity is a key component of the solution. As you learn about my Core Identity system, you will experience a mixture of feelings . . . anger, pain, happiness. Think of my system as your career mirror. Feeling unnerved, unsettled, and uncomfortable are good signs. Before making any changes in your career, you must pinpoint what needs to be changed. That's what I'm trying to help you do. You must experience emotions and benefit from them. Facing pain is necessary in order to identify solutions and motivate yourself to change your behavior. Remember cereal, eggs, and yogurt? Now you will have the opportunity to make significant career changes.

CONCEPT OF

THE CORE IDENTITY

FOCUS: PROFESSION

- One Profession
- Concurrent Different Professions
- New Profession

FUNCTION: SETTING AND SITUATION

- Status
- Role
- Industry

FOUNDATION: PASSION

- Fleeting
- Sustained

How the Core Identity System Works

There are three components to the Core Identity: *Focus, Function,* and *Foundation.* Focus and Function are the pillars; the Foundation is your passion. Your goal is the creation of a balanced Core Identity. To do that, all three—Focus, Function, and Foundation—must be the Right Fit for you and must work together synergistically. If one component of the system is the wrong fit, you will be out of balance and have a problem. The extent or magnitude of the imbalance will determine the size and significance of the problem.

What Is Focus?

Focus is the profession you choose. In your lifetime, you could have the following scenarios:

- One profession
- Concurrent different professions
- New Profession

One Profession. The forty-year career in the same organization is a thing of the past for most employees, but it is possible to have one profession. Physicians, nurses, attorneys, architects, engineers, scientists, real estate brokers, CPAs, writers, editors, and many more have one profession throughout their lives.

Begin pondering this question:
Is one profession the Right Fit for me?

Concurrent different professions. How many people do you know who have two or more different professions and practice them concurrently? I know an array of people who have risen to this challenge. One person in particular stands out in my mind. Her name is Felicia. I met her many years ago. At that time, Felicia was an actress who had a number of dramatic roles in major movies. Felicia's appearance, carriage, and voice elicited attention. She was about five feet, nine inches tall with raven black hair, porcelain skin, and piercing blue eyes that communicated her intelligence. Her rich, deep voice commanded respect. Concurrently, she was a self-employed real-estate broker selling multimillion-dollar homes in Bel Air and Beverly Hills. As a real-estate broker, she catered to the entertainment industry because, of course, she knew many people in it. Felicia juggled both professions beautifully, sometimes spending long hours on a film set and making an offer on a house on behalf of a client all in the same day. Not everyone can successfully juggle two professions, but Felicia certainly could. Before you try this approach, be sure that you can do it, too.

> Begin pondering this question:
> **Are concurrent different professions the Right Fit for me?**

New profession. What did Felicia do next? I lost track of Felicia for several years. At a chance meeting, I met a brand-new Felicia. She was no longer an actress *or* a real estate broker. During the period of time we had been out of touch, Felicia went to law school and passed the bar. In what kind of law did she specialize? Entertainment law, of course. Once more, she leveraged her entertainment contacts to generate clients. Did Felicia ever act again? No doubt she would if Steven Spielberg called her. And surely she would sell real estate again if she could represent the $300 million Aaron Spelling estate. Never throw away your professional expertise. You may need it.

> Begin pondering this question:
> **Is there a compelling reason for me to change professions?**

What Is Function?

Function is the setting, situation, and style in which you practice your profession; it includes three classifications:

- ■ Status
- ■ Role
- ■ Industry

Status. Are you an *employee* or an *entrepreneur?* As an employee you have two options: *active* or *passive*. How do you know whether you are active or passive? The hallmark of the active employee is the pursuit of performance above employer expectations. The active employee does more than what's necessary to get the job done. Remember Grace from earlier in this chapter? You can sense her enormous energy. You can envision the ways in which she actively works to exceed expectations. She says enthusiastically, "Six years later, I'm still happy in the communications industry, having added more and more responsibility each year that I've spent with my employer."

The hallmark of the passive employee is performance meant to meet the employer's basic expectations and no more. To the passive employee, it's a job, not a position of responsibility needing further commitment and nurturance. To grow your career as an employee, you must be active. If you choose to take the passive road, career satisfaction is unlikely, unless you've lowered your own expectations or standards so that you simply want and desire the minimum from yourself.

Active Employees, begin pondering this question:
**What can I do to communicate my accomplishments
to my employer?**

Passive Employees, begin pondering this question:
What can I do to motivate myself to become more active?

The term *entrepreneur* embraces a broad spectrum: independent contractors, small-business owners, and corporate moguls. Entrepreneurs are divided into two classifications: *fictitious* and *real*. Let's set the record straight. For some people, the word entrepreneur is a euphemism for "unemployed" or for finding a short-term way to generate revenue until they can find employment. And often, the "short term" turns into a long-term struggle because they are unable to become employees again, or they simply accept the minimal income they can generate. The hallmark of most fictitious entrepreneurs is a lack of commitment to growing their businesses. And like passive employees, their career satisfaction is limited.

Real entrepreneurs are committed to growing their businesses. Their bottom line is that they *do not* want to become employees again. They love the opportunity and freedom to create, grow, and expand their businesses. They no longer follow the rules of others. They forge their own destinies. The hallmark of real entrepreneurs is passion. Yet if only passion were enough, then real entrepreneurs would never fail. To succeed as an entrepreneur, the right interpersonal and technical skills are also required. In succeeding chapters, you'll learn how entrepreneurs execute the Right Fit Method to successfully grow their businesses. And in chapter seven, I'll showcase a real entrepreneur whom you will never forget. He made it big by doing it his way, as in the Frank Sinatra song.

Fictitious entrepreneurs, begin pondering this question:
What changes in my career status should I now consider?

Real entrepreneurs, begin pondering this question:
What can I do to expand my business and/or achieve more recognition?

Role. How you practice your profession is your role. You may "play" one or more roles during your lifetime, maintaining the same profession and changing the ways in which you function. Here's an example. David Downs, MD, loved medicine and children. He began his career in pediatrics working at a prestigious children's hospital in Boston. At some point, David realized that he wanted to specialize in pediatric oncology—treating children who have cancer—a shift that required him to complete additional training and pass new board exams. The next decision David needed to make was whether he wanted to join an academic medical center or a community children's hospital. He could take his choice because pediatric oncologists are in high demand.

David selected the academic medical center because his long-term goals were research and management. In his new position, he saw patients and began doing research on a rare pediatric cancer—myeloma—a primary tumor of the bone marrow. Within three years, he became the director of pediatric oncology and many years later, the hospital's medical director.

David had realized early in his career that he did not want to be a practicing physician for thirty years, and he structured his plan accordingly. To achieve his goals, he changed his *role,* not his profession, using his expertise in a new setting. He sustained his mission of helping children with pediatric cancers, implementing significant innovation in the role of medical director to achieve that goal. Like David, consider whether changing only your role and not your entire profession will satisfy your needs.

Begin pondering this question:
Should I change my role or my profession?

Industry. Is the industry in which you're working the Right Fit for you? It's important to separate your profession from the industry in which you're working. Your profession may be the Right Fit and the industry the wrong fit or vice-versa. Learn about different industries, as well as the best companies to work for within those industries. Each industry has a unique set of attributes. Find out what they are, and select the industry that suits you. Keep in mind that some employers require industry experience. Bouncing from one industry to another, without a sound rationale, may not benefit you. Investigate thoroughly before changing industries. Look before you leap! And forget the rearview mirror.

> Begin pondering this question:
> **Is my profession the Right Fit and the industry the wrong fit, or vice-versa?**

What Is Foundation?

Passion is your Foundation. Career acceleration requires passion to propel you step by step or to speed up, skipping steps on the fast track. A lack of passion will stunt your career growth. Passion is your career fuel. Make sure it's high-octane. Otherwise, it lacks power. I've observed two types of career passion: *fleeting* and *sustained.*

■ *Fleeting.* Like hummingbirds, flitting from flower to flower, people with fleeting passions take a taste and move on quickly. They believe they are deeply impassioned, but they are not. Their passion is transitory. They are unable to commit because they do not know what they want. Fleeting passion is not characteristic of the active employee or the real entrepreneur.

■ *Sustained.* True passion is sustained, functioning as the career fuel that propels you to success, either as an active employee or real entrepreneur. If you have it, you know it. Anyone who has to ask the question, "Am I passionate about my career?" is not. For some, career passion arrives early in life; for others, later; and for some, not at all. I believe it's possible to experience career passion only when your Core Identity is in balance.

> Begin pondering this question:
> **How has passion or the lack of passion influenced my career?**

The Balanced Core Identity

Are you ready to create your balanced Core Identity? I hope you have been thinking about the questions I've posed. Our goal is to pinpoint the component or components of your current Core Identity that are out of balance and to rebalance you. The creation of a balanced Core Identity is crucial to personal and professional satisfaction. It's important to remind you that you must rebalance your Core Identity before changing professions. You may be in the *right* profession and simply have issues with your Function and Foundation. Let's probe further.

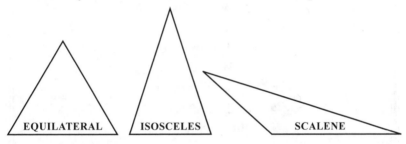

The triangle represents a balanced Core Identity. Here are three examples of the Core Identity triangles: equilateral, isosceles, and scalene. Each side represents a component of the Core Identity structure.

- *Equilateral triangle*: All sides are of equal length.
- *Isosceles triangle*: Two sides are of equal length—either the Focus and Function are weighted equally, or the Focus and Foundation, or the Function and Foundation.
- *Scalene triangle*: All sides are of different lengths—the weight of each is different.

THE CORE IDENTITY TABLE

Weighting

_____ **FOCUS: PROFESSION**
- One Profession
- Concurrent Different Professions
- New Profession

_____ **FUNCTION: SETTING AND SITUATION**
- Status
  - Employee
    - Active
    - Passive
  - Entrepreneur
    - Fictitious
    - Real
- Role
- Industry

_____ **FOUNDATION: PASSION**
- Fleeting
- Sustained

_____ **TOTAL (100%)**

Weighting the Components of the Balanced Core Identity

Now you will determine the importance of Focus, Function, and Foundation for the coming year. The outcome will become your roadmap. Remember the questions that I asked you to ponder? Think through your responses and the decisions you made. Then, study the *Core Identity Table* on page 70. Ask yourself, "Which component is of primary, secondary, and tertiary importance? Next, weight the importance of each so that all three added together equal 100 percent. For example, you may determine that Focus is 30 percent for you, Function 25 percent, and Foundation 45 percent. If all components are weighted equally, then each is 33 1/3 percent. Be sure to write each weight on the table, and make sure that the total is 100 percent. *Congratulations! You have a balanced Core Identity you are ready to implement.*

Now, look at the three triangles again, and determine which one best represents whom you want to be. Which triangle represents your balanced Core Identity?*

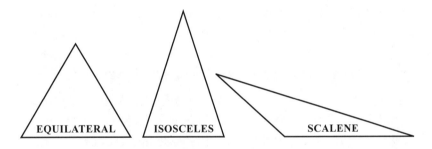

- An Equilateral triangle, with each component equaling 33 1/3 percent.
- An Isosceles triangle, in which two of the three legs are weighted the same.
- A Scalene triangle, in which all three components are weighted differently.

---

*Mathematical wizards: The angles of the isosceles and scalene triangles are purposely not considered in this scheme, which could alter your triangle's shape.

After determining which type of triangle represents your balanced Core Identity, graphically represent on the appropriate triangle the name of each component. For example, if you are an equilateral triangle, it would look like this:

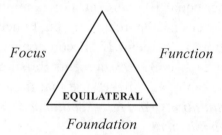

Focus   *Function*

EQUILATERAL

Foundation

It's very important that you visually see yourself in balance. Please keep this image in your mind. How do you feel? I hope you have a sense of relief and feel empowered. Many of us sit on the fence, struggling to figure out what to do with our careers. Plant your feet firmly on the ground; your balanced Core Identity is in place.

Your Annual Core Identity Checkup

Once a year, evaluate your current Core Identity to determine whether you are still in balance. To help you remember to do this, let it coincide with your annual car checkup, annual physical, or annual vacation. Add to your "annuals" the balancing of your Core Identity. Mark the date and time on your calendar. Use the *Core Identity Table* on page 74 to rebalance yourself, noting the date and time of your first annual Core Identity balancing. Please be sure to rebalance yourself annually for the rest of your professional life. Don't delay doing this important activity.

Why is it important to do your *Annual Core Identity Checkup?* Changes may have occurred in your personal and/ or professional life necessitating the rebalancing of your Core Identity. Don't ignore these changes. Identify and incorporate them into your evaluation. If you ignore the telltale signs of potential or actual problems instead of rebalancing, you could have far more to fix in the future, creating a daunting task. I believe in preventing problems rather than solving them, a philosophical approach I hope you will adopt, too.

To help keep the image of the balanced Core Identity and its significance constant in your mind, remember this Trigger Tip:

Trigger Tip
Plant your feet
firmly on the ground

Saddle-up and let's go!

FIRST ANNUAL CORE IDENTITY BALANCING

DATE _____   TIME _____

THE CORE IDENTITY TABLE

Weighting

_____ **FOCUS: PROFESSION**
- One Profession
- Concurrent Different Professions
- New Profession

_____ **FUNCTION: SETTING AND SITUATION**
- Status
  - Employee
    - Active
    - Passive
  - Entrepreneur
    - Fictitious
    - Real
- Role
- Industry

_____ **FOUNDATION: PASSION**
- Fleeting
- Sustained

_____ **TOTAL (100%)**

SECOND ANNUAL CORE IDENTITY BALANCING

DATE _____   TIME _____

THE CORE IDENTITY TABLE

Weighting

_____ **FOCUS: PROFESSION**
- One Profession
- Concurrent Different Professions
- New Profession

_____ **FUNCTION: SETTING AND SITUATION**
- Status
  - Employee
    - Active
    - Passive
  - Entrepreneur
    - Fictitious
    - Real
- Role
- Industry

_____ **FOUNDATION: PASSION**
- Fleeting
- Sustained

_____ **TOTAL (100%)**

CHAPTER FIVE

Set the Standard: Forget the Competition

Your Goal:
*Create your standard,
and establish standards.*

THE PERFORMANCE was about to begin. I gazed at an intriguing group of people sitting in front of me and asked myself, "Why do these people look familiar?" Among the group of twenty or so was a woman who was probably in her eighties. I heard her ask, "Is Steven coming?"

Then, the lights dimmed and Steven Spielberg slipped in and sat in the seat in front of me. Dressed in a black leather jacket, he was seated next to a woman I now identified as his wife, Kate Capshaw, and collectively we were about to enjoy a performance at the Geffen Playhouse in Westwood, where Spielberg is a member of the board.

At the end of the wonderful performance, the people in the Spielberg group stood. I recognized his mother among them, and she and the others were clearly delighted by what they had seen. They were hungry to hear Steven's opinion, and all eyes were glued on him as he announced, "It was just like a New York production."

Spielberg had held this Debbie Allen play to a standard of excellence akin to that of the New York theater. For him, "just like a New York production" meant "superb." We all set standards—some higher, some lower—against which we measure or evaluate something or someone. When a manufacturer creates a product aimed at meeting what is perceived to be a very high standard, the result can become a name brand—Coca Cola, Tide, Kleenex. People can become name brands just like products. Their names become the brand—Steven Spielberg, Donald Trump, and Oprah Winfrey.

What can we learn from people who become name brands? They know how to differentiate themselves from their competition, just like corporate brands. You "buy" "Spielberg," "The Donald," and "Oprah." You can do what they do. You have the capacity to *set a standard against which no one can compete.* I have planted the seed. Let the germination begin.

I was having lunch at Kay'n Dave's, a charming bistro in Westside Los Angeles whose unusual artwork on the walls includes children's drawings. The owner and I were chatting about my Win Without Competing concept, and a couple sitting nearby seemed to be listening attentively. When the owner left my table, the couple spoke up, wanting to hear more about the concept and this book. Then suddenly, the husband got up and left. But he quickly returned with a beautiful wall calendar on which I read *Doyle Gray—Ballet.* He was Doyle Gray, it turned out, the photographic artist who had created the exquisite ballet images. "These ballerinas look like paintings, not photographs," I commented, then asked Doyle, "Have you set a standard against which no one can compete?"

He answered, "Yes, I have."

A couple of weeks later, I had the opportunity to interview Doyle and was fascinated as he told me about his remarkable life. Let's bring him on stage now.

When I was three or four years old, I saw my mother constantly taking pictures. She used a black plastic Kodak Brownie camera. I wanted to use the camera. She gave me the camera with no film. Then I would pretend to take pictures. I loved to hear the click.

At age eight, I began to see that the pictures that other family members took were not framed the way I would frame them. At a family gathering, I asked my mother if I could take the pictures. She handed me the camera. When we got the pictures back, she was very impressed with my work and from that time on, I became the family photographer.

In Chicago, where I lived, I started taking pictures during the YMCA Summer Adventure Club outings and entered them in their photo contest. I knew the photo that won first prize would win when I took it. I'll describe the image—a yacht harbor with a number of sailboats tied up, with the wooden masts rising toward the gray skies. Just after it started raining, I looked through the viewfinder and snapped the picture. I told some of my friends that the picture I just took would win. At age eleven, I did indeed win my first photo award.

Years later, when I was in Vietnam with the Air Force, I was able to purchase my first 35 mm camera and several lenses. I knew that when I finished my Air Force enlistment, I wanted to pursue photography, at least as a hobby and possibly as a profession. I worked with a professional photographer in Los Angeles who became my mentor. He taught me two things: how to use different lenses and most importantly, how to use natural light.

I had an image in my head of photographing ballet students in a small studio with hardwood floors. I decided to pursue this concept and studied all of Degas's ballet work. I began to think of myself as looking over Degas's shoulder at the Paris Opera Ballet School in the 1890s. The more research I did, the more I become impassioned with Degas's approach and the entire Impressionist movement. I also studied Renoir's works and Rodin's sculptures. I began to think of myself as an impressionist photographer.

It took seven years from the time I left the Air Force to the publication of my first ballerina calendars, which will be thirty years ago in 2008. My "setting a standard" continued to evolve, and ultimately I created a style in which I photograph Degas's subject matter in Renoir's style. It's a standard against which no one can compete.

I identify deeply with Renoir and Degas, and agree strongly with Renoir's statement, "A picture must be a pleasant thing, joyous and pretty, yes, pretty. There are too many unpleasant things in life for us to fabricate more." If it was true in Renoir's time, it is certainly true today. I want to continue creating joyous images of beauty, peace, and tranquility. I see what I do as a gift.

Doyle's passion for photography and ballet compelled him to do research and set his standard very high. Competition? He never really thought about competing against others. He was aware that other photographers were focusing on ballerinas on stage, not on ballet students, as he was, and that specialization led him to differentiate himself from the competition unknowingly. He didn't fret about his competition and think about how to "conquer" his fellow photographers. He simply directed his energy toward creating an innovative technique, one that he refined until he set a standard. Doyle forgot his competition, and, in the end, Doyle Gray became a name brand in the world of ballet photography. *Doyle achieved his high standard by competing with himself, but never against others. That's what I want you to learn how to do.*

I hope you're asking yourself, "How can I become a name brand?" OR better yet, "Is it possible for me to be a 'Doyle' in my field?" Doyle worked very hard and accomplished great things because photography is the Right Fit for him. What is your niche?

Finding the Right Fit is the key, of course. Remember that thinking big will inspire you. And now I'll show you how to create a set of standards for yourself, something that's essential before you begin to search for a new opportunity.

The Blended Blueprint

Strategize to Search with Standards

Before launching into the creation of your Personal Brand, which will become the guiding force in changing your career status, it's critical to determine, as you did with your Core Identity, what is important to you right now as you seek a new position. Too often, we begin searching without a set of standards with defined criteria with which we can evaluate an opportunity. The blasting of e-mail résumés is never preceded by the fundamental question, "Is this the Right Fit for me?" Far too many talented people waste enormous amounts of time pursuing opportunities they would never accept. You must strategize before beginning your campaign.

Employees:

Put a check next to each statement that describes you.

- ☐ I hate work travel, but perhaps traveling 50 percent of the time is not too much.
- ☐ I don't want to move, but the opportunity may be worth it.

☐   I really don't want to manage people, but I do want to work for that company.

☐   I need to accept something soon, even if it's not what I want to do.

☐   I'm not sure what my minimum compensation requirements should be for my next position.

You must resolve your indecision prior to beginning your search, not after. You need what I call a Blended Blueprint, which is a set of standards that will enable you to determine which opportunities to pursue and which to let pass.

Why look at positions that are 3,000 miles away if you are very reluctant to move? Sylvia Fox, one of my client-employers, was downsized and contacted me in hopes that I could represent her. I found Sylvia a Right Fit position at an advertising agency in New Jersey and asked her whether she could move. Of course she could, she told me. She flew to the east coast for a series of interviews, her "new" employer thought she was terrific, and within days, I presented an offer to Sylvia on his behalf.

What happened next? You guessed it. Sylvia announced that she couldn't move. Her boyfriend proposed to her after she told him about the offer. Sylvia—the fox—had never mentioned to me that she had a significant other, and if she had, I certainly would have queried her carefully about whether a move was advisable, given that relationship. As I exhorted Sylvia, be honest with yourself and with others. And remember to treat others as you want to be treated yourself.

To help create your Blended Blueprint, review chapter four, paying particular attention to your balanced Core Identity. Are you an equilateral, isosceles, or scalene triangle? If you are employed and uncertain about whether you should "fix it" or "flee," completing the Blended Blueprint will provide insight into what you truly desire and whether your current employer can satisfy you or if you should actively search for a new position? **(If you are an entrepreneur, you need a Blended Blueprint, too. Running a business without careful planning could lead to failure.)**

The decisions you made about your Core Identity will help you formulate your Blended Blueprint. Take a deep breath and relax. If you have a significant other or others—including family members whose opinions you value—be sure to consult with them as you design your Blended Blueprint. You don't want to do a "Sylvia."

On the worksheet on page 85, I've identified four categories for which I want you to develop criteria, establishing a standard for each category. Reflect on each, then express your thoughts in writing on the worksheet. There is additional space for you to add categories that are important to you—schools, children, horses, and boats are examples of special needs and concerns. What issues are specific to you?

Before you embark on your journey of discovery to create the Blended Blueprint: Worksheet, please read carefully "Establishing Criteria." You need to determine what is really important to you in order to pursue the Right Fit position.

Establishing Criteria

Position: Think about the position you want to pursue. Remember to ask yourself whether you have the qualifications for that position. Would an employer see you as the Right Fit, matching the key components of the specs?

If you don't like to manage people, then do not list a management title. You may be an outstanding monetary economist but unwilling and/or unable to effectively oversee other economists. **(Entrepreneurs who intend to grow their groups should plan to hire managers, so that they can use their time wisely to do what only they can do.)**

Industry: If you like the industry in which you currently have experience, that's great. If you want to change your role within the same industry, it can be done, but some changes are more difficult than others. Before deciding to make this type of change, you should do research to determine the feasibility of doing so. For example, a hospital that intends to hire a new pharmacist usually wants him or her to have experience working in a hospital, not a drugstore. Can you overcome the employer's objection if you are a drugstore pharmacist wanting to change to the hospital setting? It's possible to do so, but not easy. Be careful not to make assumptions about potential employers' willingness to change their specs.

If you want to switch to a different industry, it's possible but, again, you will need to overcome employer objections, unless the employer is searching for someone outside the given industry. **(Entrepreneurs must determine who their client base is and target those markets accordingly.)**

Location: Decide whether you're willing to move and, if you are, determine which geographic locations are acceptable to you and your significant others. If you are accustomed to an urban environment, you may not be able to adjust to a rural area, for example. Know thyself! **(Entrepreneurs should carefully select the right location for their business, thinking about whether they may need to expand to other offices to serve their clients.)**

Compensation: You must determine the *minimum* compensation package you will accept. Break it down into components: base salary, bonus (if applicable), commission (if applicable), stock or stock options (if applicable), and benefits. If you want a position that pays a base salary of $100,000 and your goal is realistic, then that's what you should pursue. If you settle for what you don't want, you will not be happy. **(Entrepreneurs need to be especially careful to plan for "dry periods." If you do not have the financial acumen to**

manage your finances, you must hire the financial experts to do what you can't do. Don't wing it!)

THE BLENDED BLUEPRINT: WORKSHEET

Describe in detail your next career move. Be specific. Create a set of criteria to help you establish standards against which you can measure a potential new opportunity.

Position

Industry

Location

Compensation

———

———

———

———

How did you enjoy your journey of exploring what's important to you in seeking a new position or growing your business? I hope you spent time talking with others who are close to you and made substantive decisions. Planning with this blueprint will save you a lot of time and help prevent you from pursuing some very wrong fits.

It's now time to create your Blended Blueprint. *Return to the Blended Blueprint: Worksheet on page 85. Review your worksheet and then, on the Blended Blueprint following, determine for yourself the importance of each category—expressed as a percentage—so the total equals 100 percent.* If you included additional categories on your worksheet, add them to the blueprint. I strongly recommend not weighting each one equally. You must prioritize them so that it's clear to you what's more important and less important to you. This will help you make decisions, as we proceed.

THE BLENDED BLUEPRINT	
Weighting	**Criteria**
_____	Position
_____	Industry
_____	Location
_____	Compensation
_____	_____
_____	_____
_____	_____
_____	_____
_____	**Total (100%)**

Be specific as you describe the criteria. For example, under "Location" you could write "No relocation" or "Urban, northeastern U.S. only, prefer Boston but other cities are acceptable (family and significant others agree)."

(Entrepreneurs should list specific locations, if planning expansion.)

After you finish considering the percentages, be sure to discuss the Blended Blueprint again with those who have given you input into the worksheet. They are likely to see things a bit differently from you. Finalize the Blended Blueprint, then *plant your feet firmly on the ground,* as you did when you finished the Core Identity. I recommend standing up and really planting your feet. Try it. It will give you a feeling of power.

Trigger Tip
Set the standard

Onward and upward!

CHAPTER SIX

Shaping Your Brand: the Right Fit

Your Goal:
Master the match.

THE CONCEPT of the match is a complex one. The Blended Blueprint incorporates a set of weighted standards with which you will gauge potential positions to determine whether they should be filed under "investigate further" or "discard." To win a position whose specs coincide with your own requires matching across a broad spectrum of categories.

After you begin your new position, you need to keep matching and rematching yourself to reinforce or change the fit. **(After capturing clients, entrepreneurs constantly need to reinforce the match to keep the clients they want and let go of those clients who are no longer the Right Fit.)**

To demonstrate the inner workings of matching and rematching, I asked Jason Moreno, age thirty-two, a highly successful entrepreneur, to look back at his career, beginning with his first position as an active employee. When I first met Jason, I found his style and determination intriguing. My company and his are housed in the same office building, one that caters to entrepreneurs, and I've watched him create his empire firsthand. **Please welcome Jason onto our stage, and immerse yourself in his story—soak up his passion, determination, and wisdom.**

I quickly ripped off my suit and tie in the bathroom of UCLA's Career Center. I knew that my intramural basketball team was counting on me, and I had to change and get to the courts across campus in less than seven minutes. As I rushed out of the bathroom and down the hallway, I almost ran over the woman who had spent the last hour interviewing me. She had come out of the interview room to get some water and was shocked to see me in a T-shirt and shorts, because only three minutes ago, I was in my one and only blue suit, trying to impress her in my first-ever professional interview. I sheepishly grinned and mentioned that it was the semi-finals and kept on running.

I was extremely disappointed that I had ruined my first grown-up interview. It was the middle of my junior year at UCLA and the Big 6 (now Big 4) accounting firms were on campus interviewing applicants for summer internships. My top choice was Deloitte and Touche, but I knew that they only took two UCLA students out of the sixty that applied. I felt the interview went pretty well—it was more of a conversation than an inquisition—but running over the recruiter had to count against me. I was already on the fence, I felt, by having a 3.4 GPA compared to the 4.0s that were interviewing alongside me. Regardless, I still wanted it. I had never left an interview without getting the job. Of course, these other jobs were fast food and UCLA student store positions, but I had a perfect track record, one I was afraid was about to be broken.

The next morning at 7:00 a.m., my phone rang. I had learned by my junior year not to take any classes before noon, so this startled me. I groggily grabbed the receiver and barked out an annoyed, "hello."

"Jason, it's Mary, the recruiter at Deloitte. I wanted to get in touch with you immediately to let you know that you are our top candidate for the summer internship. Can you come down to the office next week to meet a few more people? If all goes well, I want to extend you an offer for a summer internship."

It took me a minute to process this information, but eventually a smile came across my face. I had learned, in this moment, a lesson that would repeat itself over and over in my career: *Charisma goes further than talent.* I was definitely not the best accountant who applied for the position, but my interpersonal skills, my ability to communicate, and maybe even my loyalty to my basketball team proved to Deloitte that I was someone they wanted to put in front of their clients. Deloitte already knew what I found out that day: Accounting could be taught, charisma could not.

I enjoyed my summer internship and learned a lot about the business world. I accepted a full-time offer shortly after that summer and was able to relax during my senior year. Okay, maybe not relax, but it was one less headache. I spent the end of my senior year preparing for the CPA exam. The CPA exam is a 2-day, 16-hour, gut-wrencher that less than 8 percent of the test-takers pass. I enjoyed learning from my UCLA professors about the strategies to pass the exam and really put my mind to studying for it. I took the test at the end of my college career and got the news that summer that I had passed it in full. I was excited, but it was expected. Everyone who knew me, knew that I would pass. Even my professors had no doubt that I would be successful. I was the only one who appeared to be unsure. That is when I realized my next lesson in business (and life): *The price of potential is the burden of expectation.* Throughout my career, everyone has expected me to succeed with every chance I took, so I never really exceeded anyone's expectations. My success was always the expected, the norm, the given. I guess for most people, this is a compliment.

I started at Deloitte as a bright-eyed staff accountant ready to change the world. It was only a few weeks into the job that I realized that a hundred-thousand person company had more bureaucracy than I could handle. While I enjoyed doing audits of different companies in an array of industries, I didn't appreciate taking orders from senior accountants who were my bosses only because they were a year older than I was. I learned that in large companies there is an "up or out" mentality that you can't get away from. My partner-advisor was a bright woman whom I really respected, and she laid it out for me: "The D and F students get fired; the A and B students move on to do bigger, better things; the C students hang around and keep getting promoted until they eventually make partner." This was not for me.

I knew that I wanted my CPA designation, and a requirement of getting that certificate was that I work at an accounting firm for two years. Knowing that my hands were tied for a while, I made the best of my situation. I spent one year in tax and one year in audit, learning anything and everything I could about the business world. I wasn't sure where I was going to end up, but I wanted to know what my options were. Deloitte was very flexible in giving me the clients that I wanted, but they couldn't fix the fact that some of my seniors were not people from whom I could learn.

Very quickly, Jason determined that Deloitte was not the Right Fit for the long term, and that he could not fix the fit. It's remarkable that at age twenty-three, Jason figured out exactly what did not meet his needs and standards. Let's see what Jason decided to do next.

Since I wasn't fully challenged at Deloitte, I went back to my UCLA professors and asked about teaching for the CPA exam. I had tutored students for a number of my teachers during my time at UCLA, so they knew my teaching skills were solid. I was recommended for the position and given one shot to get the job. I was asked to prepare a four-hour lecture and present it with one of my professors sitting in the back of the room. At break time, if I wasn't doing well, my professor would pull me and complete the class himself. Needless to say, it was a lot of pressure.

These students had been lectured by seasoned UCLA professors, and now I was up on stage, younger than half the class, trying to convince them that I was just as good, if not better, than their other teachers. I prepped over forty hours for that four-hour lecture because I wanted to look good. I was worried during the first hour because the class took some time to warm up to me, but at the break my professor pulled me aside and said I was doing great, and then he left the class to me. I was excited to get the job, but I also had expected it. *Expect Success* is something I had always told myself. If I was prepared, I should expect success in everything I did. Too many people expect the worst, so that they are never disappointed. This defeatist attitude will get you nowhere in life. If you plan ahead, prepare, and execute, there is no reason you shouldn't reap the benefits of success.

Deloitte was very amenable to my teaching the CPA review. They liked the free marketing they got when I announced my affiliation to the class. I liked being able to do something beyond basic accounting and to develop my teaching skills. The only issue I had with this position was the timing. Classes were from 6:00 to 10:00 p.m. on weekdays and 8:00 a.m. to 5:00 p.m. on weekends. I would get into work at Deloitte at 6:00 a.m. so I could put in a full day before I had to leave to teach. Some nights, I'd come back to the office at 10:00 p.m., after my class was done, to finish up any open assignment. I took on *way* too much work at Deloitte, but I had to learn as much as I could while I was there, and a forty-hour week just wasn't going to cut it. On days when I'd go back to work after a class and work until 5:00 a.m., I couldn't help but question my decision. On those mornings, I'd leave the office at 5:00 a.m. to get home in time to take a shower, put on a new suit, and beat traffic back to the office. It was a little out of control, but I learned so much that would help me later on.

I excelled at teaching because my charisma and intelligence seemed to blend together beautifully for the job. It was a real high to go back to UCLA and teach in the classrooms where I had been a student only twelve months earlier. When I received my first set of evaluations and saw that I was rated higher than most of my professors, I knew I had come to my true calling. I loved to teach. So, maybe I should follow this dream and become a teacher?

This decision weighed on me very heavily. I loved the business world, but I loved to teach as well. I looked into PhD programs and the time commitments required. I learned that a full-time professorship was less about teaching and more about research and publishing. While I valued research highly, it's not where I wanted to spend my time, so my dream of becoming a full-time professor ended.

Jason investigated a teaching career at the university level and realized that this would not be the Right Fit for him. He recognized that the Core Identity he thought he wanted was wrong for him. Therefore, he didn't pursue a PhD. He searched further to discover his Core Identity.

As I was reaching the magical "two-year" mark at Deloitte, I knew it was time to start looking around. No sooner had I put together my résumé than I got a call from one of my old students at UCLA. He told me that his older brother had started up a new dot.com company and had interviewed twenty-six controllers and couldn't find one who could fit in and do the job. I was twenty-three years old and not yet ready to be a controller, but I took a shot and interviewed with his brother, the CEO. I must have impressed him because he offered me the job, and I became employee number eight at Mobile Automation. I was the only financial person at the company, so I played the role of accounting clerk and CFO as well.

I was excited to begin a new venture and looked forward to the fast-paced start-up world. On day one, however, I learned very quickly that I was in over my head. The VP of marketing called me into her office and started ranting about burn rates and expense variances. I had heard these terms before, but didn't know what to make of them in the real world. The company was in an audit by Price Waterhouse Coopers (PWC), and the partner called me up to discuss the issue of stock option expensing. I was baffled by the terms he was using and thought I'd made a *huge* mistake in taking the position on. What the hell did I know about this? It would have been so much easier if I had stayed at Deloitte. But, instead of flipping out, I put the partner on hold, and called my old Deloitte partner-advisor on line two. I asked her what the heck this guy meant and what my response should be. She gave me some sound advice, and I went back to line one and regurgitated it to the PWC partner. He bought it hook, line, and sinker, and the call was over. I wasn't ready for this position yet, but at least I knew that I had a valuable network of resources to call on when I was in trouble.

I spent the next year not only as the sole financial person, but also as the de-facto lawyer of the company. We had tech people and sales people, but since I was the controller, I was in charge of all contracts and negotiations. I was totally unprepared for this as well, but I loved every minute of it. I was getting the greatest education I could, *and* getting paid for it. The company needed to come up with a round of funding, and they turned to me. I'm not sure how I raised $2.5 million, negotiated the terms of the deal, and wrote the purchase agreement, but someone had to do it. My feet were to the fire, and I had put as much time in as necessary to complete the tasks I took on. I was working more hours here than at Deloitte, but I knew the things I learned were valuable.

I convinced the CEO to allow me to be the secretary of the company, so I could sit in on the board meetings. I got to see the bigwigs in action and learn how the real decisions were made. In the first meeting I attended, I sat between two of our investors. I will never forget their conversation. They were chatting about which helicopter to buy. I was just starting to pay off student loans, and these guys were spending millions buying helicopters. I was in over my head, but I wouldn't have had it any other way.

After a year at Mobile Automation, our VP of sales just wasn't cutting it. I could see it and presented this information to the CEO. I wanted the company to succeed, so I felt it was my fiduciary duty to bring this issue up. The CEO agreed with me, but said that we had no other options at this time because it would take too long to search, hire, and train a replacement.

I wasn't happy with his answer, so I responded the only way I knew how. I told him that I could run sales. He reminded me that I had no experience doing this, which was true, but I had seen the company from every angle and I wanted the chance to do more. Well, he gave me the chance, and soon my double life began. I was VP of sales from 8:00 a.m. to 5:00 p.m., and then when the sales team left at 5:00,

I put on my controller hat to start my second job. I had never felt so invigorated. I was doing this for the education, but also for the potential revenue. I had been granted stock options when I was hired and was awarded more when I ran the sales team. If the company took off, I'd be a millionaire and ready to retire at twenty-five! The company eventually hired someone to handle sales, but the few months that I ran the department were very eye-opening for me. Managing salespeople was much different from directing any other type of employee. A good salesperson is an adrenaline junky who gets his fix from his last sale, but he's only as good as that last sale. This was not a career I wanted to pursue, but it was great to learn about it.

The technology that Mobile Automation developed—laptop management for IT professionals—was a bit ahead of its time. CIOs thought it was interesting, but they weren't ready to open their pocketbooks yet. I could see the writing on the wall and cash slipping away from the company, which suggested downsizing. It was the right call, but it's never easy when you have to let go of some of your closest friends. The night before the layoffs, I couldn't sleep, and the day of the firings was as unpleasant a day as I had ever experienced. I think I handled it with class and dignity, though, and was actually commended by some of the people I had let go. Unfortunately, it was a stopgap solution, because four months later I had to go through another round of layoffs. This time, I called my own number, because that was the best decision for the company. My friends and family couldn't believe that I was laying myself off, but my job was to do what was best for the company, and that didn't involve me in my position in the future. It was another dreadful day that I will never forget.

It turns out it *was* the right move for the company, because six years later it was sold for $20 million. I don't regret leaving; the other opportunities I took on helped me

build the portfolio of knowledge that I would put to use
when I started my own company.

Jason was constantly learning and re-evaluating his Core
Identity, preparing himself to identify and create the Right Fit.
In the midst of his company's crisis, he downsized himself for
the good of the company. *Would you fire yourself?*

As I looked for my next job, I was starting to get the feel
for what I wanted in a company. I wanted fast pace, I wanted
the entrepreneurial spirit, but I also wanted solid financial
backing so that my paycheck wouldn't be in jeopardy. I
found all of those at an idealab! "incubator" company called
Firstlook.com, which was an innovator in streaming media
on the web. idealab! was the talk of the town because they
had set up some of the greatest dot.com success stories at
the time, such as Etoys and Goto.com. The company I joined
had received first-round funding from the top-notch venture capital firm in Silicon Valley, Kleiner Perkins. At the
time, the company had an interim CFO who interviewed
me for the position. He found it hard to believe I was only
twenty-four, given everything that my résumé listed. I think
he assumed I was exaggerating and called me out on many
of the bullet points. I calmly described what I did and how
I did it and he sat in awe. "But how did you know how to
do any of this?" he repeatedly asked. "I didn't," I replied,
"but it had to get done, so I stepped up and learned how to
do it." Another interview, another job offer. I was still bat-
ting 1,000.

I came in as the twelfth employee and worked closely
with the CEO to help build the company. We grew very
quickly. Since I was the finance team, I also became the
human resources team. I knew nothing of human resources,
but once again, with my feet to the fire, I had to learn, so I
did. I was hiring as many as forty people a month, and our

company was growing exactly like we had planned. We went out for more financing and I led the way. Our CEO and COO had not raised financing before, but I had, so I taught them the ins and outs and what to look for in a term sheet. We finished our round of funding with $50 million from more top-tier investors. We were riding high, and I was a millionaire on paper. Our board meetings, which, once again, I attended as the corporate secretary, were full of hi-tech displays and promises of success. I sat next to the head of idealab!, Bill Gross, and was amazed at his entrepreneurial prowess as well as the millions of dollars his other companies were making after they had gone public. Firstlook.com was on the same track, and I was looking to cash out soon. I put in eighty-ninety hours a week at Firstlook, just like everyone else. We all had the common goal of success, as well as the hope of riches. Working this around my CPA teaching schedule was tricky, but I made it work. I wanted the financial rewards that some of my neighboring idealab! companies were achieving.

Firstlook.com was the first to bring streaming media to the Internet in the form of movie and videogame previews. People would click on a popular movie to see a two-minute theatrical trailer and learn more about it. The only problem was that we weren't monetizing these clicks. We were getting a ton of traffic to our site, which is what the investors wanted, but we weren't turning it into significant revenue. I brought this up at a board meeting and was told, "It doesn't matter now about revenue. We're trying to build a brand and get customer retention. Once we get those, then we'll worry about revenue." I didn't love this answer, but I was only twenty-five years old, and these people were seasoned veterans who had millions of dollars of investment money at their disposal. Surely they must know what they're doing, I thought. As time went on and cash flow remained negative, I went to my CEO and explained that negative gross margins just don't work. You can't "make it up on volume" if everything you're selling is being sold at a loss. But he was too caught up in the hype that the press was giving us—we were being crowned the king of streaming media—so nothing else seemed to matter.

All of this changed in March 2000. The market crashed as the Internet bubble burst. We were in line for an IPO later in the year, but those plans were immediately squashed. The market had appreciated our website, which drew six million hits per day, but now they were looking for companies that made money off of those eyeballs, and we weren't one of them. Again, I had to lay off 25 percent of my staff, and it was not easy. I had personally hired a lot of these people, and I had to tell them that our plan was all wrong. The company tried to reposition itself, but in January 2001, I saw the writing on the wall and suggested another group of layoffs, once again adding myself to the list. It was a fun ride, but the "new Internet world" bowed down to the old-school metrics I had learned about at UCLA. Tried and true methods were successful for a reason, while negative margins were always a bad idea.

I spent the next few months figuring out what to do. I was jaded. I had put my heart and soul into ninety-hour weeks only to have everything topple down around me. I wasn't alone, either. My other dot.com buddies and I would get together for lunch often and try to figure out the next steps. There wasn't a right answer. We had been in an environment where ideas flowed freely, and working till midnight was fine, as long as you could get a game of football or darts in, and riches were on the horizon. We had the potential for the perfect job, but it all crashed down around us.

I had to find a company that would be open and flexible, like the dot.coms, but still have a solid business model that would survive market fluctuations. I interviewed at a few different companies and didn't like any of them. I was told by one HR person that the CEO had a closed-door policy and wasn't interested in hearing ideas from his staff. I got up immediately to walk out of the interview, and she was perplexed. "Don't you want to meet him and learn more about the company?" I laughed and tried to explain, but she was baffled and so I left. I received a couple of job offers in my hunt, but they were all just marginal positions. Nothing really interested me, and I knew that I needed a paycheck soon. I was trying to figure out which mediocre position with which marginal company to accept until I had a moment of clarity.

Never Settle. It came to me like a bullet. I was about to take on a job I didn't care about for a company that was meaningless to me. Where was the benefit in that? I had never been the noiseless drone who carries on all day long just for a paycheck, and I wasn't going to start now. I turned down all the open offers and rethought my plan.

Jason had embarked on a journey of discovery to figure out the Right Fit for him. To do that, he held an array of positions in a variety of companies. Focusing on his guiding principle, *"Never Settle,"* Jason ultimately decided that working for others was not the Right Fit for him. At that moment, an entrepreneur was born.

At the beginning of your career, you are a blushing bride or groom, eager to get that first job. Understanding the Right Fit may be difficult if you do not have enough work and life experience. Using the Right Fit Method will guide you early on and throughout your career to help you determine whether the position is the Right Fit for you, reducing the need to take many positions to figure it out. Employing the standards that he created, Jason took a career step that changed his life, which I will share with you in chapter twelve.

Steps to Success

Right now, I hope you're feeling fantastic, readying yourself to create your Personal Brand. Let's check to be sure that you've mastered the basics.

Mastering the Basics

Put a plus (+) next to each statement that describes you now. If you need to improve, put a checkmark (√).

		+	√
Chapter 2	■ I make fewer assumptions, continuing to reduce the number of assumptions that I make.	____	____
Chapter 3	■ I consciously change my behavior, which makes me more effective in my personal and professional life.	____	____
Chapter 4	■ My new Core Identity has helped me to target what my next career step should be.	____	____
Chapter 5	■ My Blended Blueprint gives me the standards that I need to figure out which opportunities to pursue.	____	____
Chapter 5	■ Setting a standard against which no one can compete will replace my old-style competitive mindset.	____	____

If you need to do more work on one or more of the basics, please review the relevant chapters. We must be sure you're ready to hit the ground running, and to do so, mastering these fundamentals is essential. Once they become part of your professional arsenal, fashioning and demonstrating your Personal Brand will become part of an evolutionary process.

Your Personal Brand

The Right Fit

The creation of the Right Fit is the first step of your Personal Brand. In chapters 7 and 8, I will discuss the second and third steps in creating your Personal Brand—Package to Pitch and Manage the Process. **(Entrepreneurs: The concept of your Personal Brand is suitable for entrepreneurs as well as employees. The difference is that you are matching your specs to those of your clients, rather than employers. Extract that which is relevant to your own needs, adapting and applying accordingly.)** The number of Personal Brands you can create is endless. Your Personal Brand must match the specific opportunity you are pursuing. Let's see how this works.

Imagine: You have decided to seek a new position. In front of you sits a sea of potential opportunities. You stop yourself from blasting your résumé into cyberspace or posting yourself on a website, waiting for responses. Instead, you carefully evaluate each opportunity to determine whether the fit is right for you. Gather the "sea" and place all the opportunities it yields on your desk. Create three piles: pursue, discard, and investigate.

To evaluate the fit of each one, ask yourself: Does this opportunity match my Core Identity and Blended Blueprint? Then, if there is:

$$
\begin{array}{rcl}
\text{No Match} & \rightarrow & \text{Discard} \\
\text{Match} & \rightarrow & \text{Pursue} \\
\text{Need More Info} & \rightarrow & \text{Investigate}
\end{array}
$$

Look into those opportunities whose descriptions are incomplete, if they particularly interest you. Perhaps a friend described something and didn't have all the details, or a posted ad is vague, which is not uncommon.

Interpreting the Employer's Perspective

Now we need to evaluate the "pursue" choices from the employer's perspective. Are you the Right Fit for the employer? Because you understand the value of weighting components, you also need to know, "What is the relative importance of each requirement the employer has articulated?" But chances are good that you do not know. That's why you don't want to send your résumé to an employer until you have spoken with someone within the organization who *does* know. When you have that conversation, you may also find out that the company is "feeling its way" toward finding the fit, which means that their standards and weightings for the match are probably unclear at the moment. In chapter 7, "Selling Your Brand: Package to Pitch," I'll help you clarify and flush out the fit, using the new information you gather to your advantage.

But first, let's look at a posting and determine whether you fit, using *only* the information we currently have. We'll find out whether the match is strong enough to warrant the writing of a résumé to match the specs, a résumé that demonstrates your Right Fit Personal Brand.

Employer's Perspective

***P**lease sit down at your desk* and make yourself comfortable. Have a snack and beverage, if you like. From your "pursue" pile, pick a position you would love to have. Then, use the following guidelines to begin evaluating it.

1. Look at the title of the position and its description. Ask yourself, "Do I match the profession, level of responsibility, and career progression?" Sometimes, the level is incorporated in the title, but often it is not. For example, if your specialty is finance and you want to become a chief financial officer (CFO), check to see if you must have already held this position elsewhere or if the company is looking for someone who is ready to be promoted into that position. If you are already a CFO, be sure the company wants an experienced CFO. Career progression is a significant factor. Some companies are very particular about progression. They have in mind the step-by-step positions that the ideal candidate should have held. If, for example, you have bounced back and forth between higher and lower positions, you may be hoisting a red flag. Read the posting carefully if you are a "red flagger" and consider whether your qualifications are strong enough to overcome this objection.

2. Look at required degrees, certifications, and licenses. Read these requirements carefully. Determine if there is an education requirement and whether it is preferred or required. "Preferred" means that the employer would like the candidate to have a specific degree or certification, such as MBA or CPA. "Required" for many employers means mandatory, but sometimes the employers are flexible. If, for example, an MBA is a requirement for a position and you have nearly completed that degree, the employer could waive the requirement, provided your experience is strong enough.

3. Look at the years of experience the posting calls for, an indicator of the seasoning that the company desires and a hint at the salary range that it has in mind. If ten years of experience are required and you have only three years, it's highly unlikely that you can create a pitch to overcome this objection—unless you're a "Jason." If, however, you have seven or eight years of experience, as long as you match on the other key criteria, your pitch can work.

As for salary range, if you are currently earning $60,000 a year and the range for the position is $150,000–$175,000, you are the wrong fit from the employer's perspective. Do not waste your time. If the salary range is not stated, it should be implied. Look for indicators, such as the size of the company, magnitude of responsibility, and the number of employees requiring supervision, if this is a management position. Use these factors to gauge the salary range, which is indicative of the employer's expectations for the Right Fit candidate.

4. Examine the industry-experience requirements. If specific industries are named and the posting explicitly states that experience in one or more such industries is required, pay careful attention to this. The lack of required industry experience is not an easy objection to overcome, unless you have worked in industries that are similar and you can demonstrate that relationship. Don't assume that the employer already sees the similarity. You must show it.

5. Look at management. If this is a management position and you have absolutely no management experience, whether you can overcome that shortcoming depends on a number of factors. Remember Laurie? She had very little management experience, and it wasn't recent. The position she sought—dean of a college at a university—required significant management experience for the successful oversight of faculty. Note that I didn't use the word "manage." Laurie's pitch convinced the university officials that they needed someone to *oversee* the faculty, not manage them. She explained as she was interviewed that faculty require a certain level of independence, and that she would respect that need. She demonstrated her understanding of the faculty mindset, which ended the inquiries about her management experience. Just as Laurie did, you will need to determine whether your pitch can overcome the management objection, if you lack that experience.

Pursue?

I want you to do a preliminary evaluation. Until you speak with the employer, you cannot conclusively determine whether you are the Right Fit. At this moment, you do not have enough information to make that decision.

With each of the five evaluation questions I've discussed, I have focused on the match from the perspective of what's missing. Do your qualifications appear to match 80 percent of the standards? If they do, then it's possible to develop a pitch that will overcome what's missing—as long as your other qualifications are strong enough, the employer is flexible, and your pitch is right on the mark. Having said that, you must be realistic. In some situations, the employer views certain requirements as mandatory and simply will not budge. That's why

I'll show you in the next chapter how to do some sleuthing before spending lots of time preparing a résumé that will be instantly discarded. You will learn how to probe the employer to find out what's most important to the employer and, based on that information, whether you should pursue the opportunity. You don't want to waste your time if you are not the Right Fit. If the employer is uncertain about the standards of the fit and is looking at many candidates to help figure it out, your Right Fit pitch may be the turning point in your favor.

The Time of Reckoning

Think through the five evaluation questions I have given you, and as you do, consider the feasibility of overcoming potential objections with your pitch. Evaluate your fit and determine if you are:

- 100 percent the Right Fit, with no obvious objections to overcome,
- 80 percent or more the Right Fit, with objections to overcome,
- The Wrong Fit, plain and simple, and the opportunity has to be discarded.

If you discarded the opportunity, return to your "pursue" pile and evaluate another. You need to identify two opportunities: one for which you are exactly the Right Fit (100 percent), and another with which you can fix the fit (80 percent or more). Soon, you will become an expert evaluator and quickly select the right opportunities to pursue.

Pursue!

Now, you will create a résumé for the position you evaluated as "100 percent the Right Fit." Set the other position aside and work with it, after you master the Right Fit Method.

Your Right Fit Résumé

This is not just a résumé. It's *your* résumé, showing your Personal Brand—the exquisite fit between you, the employer, and the position. It's not an off-the-rack document. Your résumé is tailor-made. It must differentiate you from other candidates who seek the same position. *Your résumé must set the standard against which no one else can compete.* How? The résumé must be self-contained, and it must clearly tell the story of the exquisite fit. Don't tell the story in a cover letter—that's too risky. If a cover letter is lost and you have supplied only a generic résumé, the fit will be lost as well. Moreover, employers like to examine résumés. They're easier to digest than letters.

Envision the résumé as a first glimpse of you. You want to make a strong, distinctive, and positive impression, just as you would in person. Your résumé needs to be "well dressed," its layout well designed. If graphic design is not your forte, consult with someone who can ably assist you in making it eye-catching and easy to read, ensuring that it quickly reinforces your fit with the employer. Select typefaces that are distinctive, but not strange. Use a bulleted format, and employ bold and italic type to highlight what the employer should read immediately. It's up to you to show the fit, not for the employer to figure it out. Step by step, you must show how perfectly you match the position. Because you're creating a résumé for a position for which you're a 100 percent fit, this should be easy to do.

Consider carefully these matching tips, which include common employer objections and how to overcome them.

■ Résumé Length
Don't make the erroneous assumption that your résumé must contain a certain number of pages—unless this is an employer or industry requirement. You need to show how and

why you fit the position. Use precisely the number of pages you need to communicate the message, eliminating unnecessary information, including career information from far in the past.

■ Positions Held

For each position you have held, write only two or three lines explaining what your responsibilities were. *Your focus should be on outcome—what you achieved while you held that position—not on process.* Let's look at a simple example. An author states in his résumé that he has written thirty nonfiction books. That's the process. What has he achieved? Twenty-five books have been published, and three of them were *New York Times* bestsellers. That's the outcome.

■ Education

If specific degrees, certifications, or licenses are required, and you have them now or you can state the dates on which you will have them, place your education credentials at the beginning of the résumé. If you do not match the education requirement precisely, place your education information at the résumé's end. Be sure that if you lack a particular education requirement, your experience is strong enough to overcome the expected objection. If you do not want to disclose your age, then omit dates after your degrees, certifications, or licenses, unless your profession requires disclosure.

■ Honors

Be sure to include all the honors you have received. Usually, honors are listed with education. If you have many of them, select those that are the Right Fit for this opportunity.

■ Short Stints

If you have changed jobs frequently, you must overcome this objection. I define frequently as switching to something new every year or two. If you have remained in the same profession and industry and were a victim of downsizing, clearly state why with *each* downsizing. For example: *Reason for leaving: Downsized, resulting from a company merger.* Be very specific about why you were downsized. If you have changed professions and fields frequently because you have not had a satisfying Core Identity until now, your résumé is not the right place to explain this. This you must do in person.

■ Dates of Employment

To emphasize longevity, place the dates you were employed on either side of the page, in a vertical column. Employers like stability, so let them see your stability quickly. If, on the other hand, you have had many short stints, or a mixture of short and long, you can embed the dates next to each position. For example:

Director of Sales (2006–2007)
Happy Days Corporation
Houston, Texas

Be sure to begin your chronological career history from the present, even if you are writing a curriculum vitae. Our society focuses on *now!*

■ Time Period

Deciding how far back to trace your career is dependent upon many factors, including your age, the level of the position, and the employer's requirements. If you have thirty or more years of experience, list your work history only for the past ten or fifteen years, unless it's necessary to add more years to show your career progression. Your goal is to demonstrate the fit. At the interview, you can share more, if you determine it's appropriate to do so.

■ Research

Visit the employer's website and use other resources to learn as much as you can about the company. You want to identify specific details that are not necessarily articulated in the position description. Try to determine where you match the employer in areas that aren't discussed in the position description. If your target company is large and you have worked for companies of similar size, show this on your résumé. Don't assume the employer knows your previous company's size, unless it is one of the Fortune 500. For example:

The Right Fit Company (16,000 employees)
Los Angeles, CA

■ Photos

Do *not* include your photo on your résumé. Leave a little to the employer's imagination.

■ Spelling

No spelling errors!

■ Résumé Paper

Select white, ivory, or light beige paper with a good weight and a feeling of substance.

Now you're ready to design your Right Fit résumé, incorporating my success secrets in working with hundreds of candidates. By design, I am not providing a model résumé for you to copy because I want *you* to *think* about how to design your résumé to match the specific position. There is no ready-made template, nor should there be.

Beginning with "positions held," take each point and follow my directions. Think of your résumé as a puzzle and each matching entry as a piece of the puzzle. After ensuring that each matching point meets my guidelines, put each piece in place, carefully laying out your résumé and making sure it is visually pleasing and easy to read.

When it's complete, evaluate your résumé to determine whether you have created a 100 percent Right Fit résumé that *sets a standard against which no one can compete.* Ask yourself these questions:

1. Does the overall appearance of the résumé invite the employer to read it?
2. Is the match between my background, experience, and the position description clearly articulated so that a non-expert in my field can comprehend the fit point by point?
3. Have I eliminated all the objections that I can identify?

If you answered "yes" to all three questions, you are approaching the standard. To reach the standard, you must learn still more from the employer about the match in order to overcome all possible objections, which you can address by revising your résumé.

You should be feeling good. You're mastering the match, and changing your behavior as you do so. Your Right Fit résumé will be ready to "road test" shortly. Until then, be patient. Your goal is to apply for fewer positions, selecting only the Right Fit opportunities—and winning.

Trigger Tip
Eliminate hiring objections

Let's get ready for the road test!

CHAPTER SEVEN

Selling Your Brand: Package to Pitch

Your Goal:
Master the broadcast.
Pick, Probe, and Pitch.

CREATING THE PERFECT PITCH to demonstrate how you fit a position may sound easy, but it's not. Your Right Fit résumé is your written pitch. Yet it's important not to send it to a prospective employer, because ads and even detailed position descriptions rarely provide enough information to articulate the fit. Why? Let's let Laurie share her assumptions and explain:

Her first assumption: "I thought employers would know what they were looking for in a candidate."
But actually: "They did not."

Her second assumption: "I thought they would provide me with all the information I would need to know."

115

But actually: "I spent hours and hours downloading from the web, and I still had to ask them to send me information."

Her third assumption: "I thought they would know whom they wanted me to see and when."

But actually: "They asked *me!* They didn't know. I e-mailed and phoned and said whom I'd like to see."

It's all too easy to assume that a prospective employer has developed a careful blueprint of the Right Fit for a specific position, managing all the aspects of the interview process. Yet if Laurie and I had not been working together, she might have given up. She was frustrated, and I showed her repeatedly how to turn the employer's flexibility to her advantage—how to view the employer's lack of clarity as a positive, rather than a negative. Consider vagueness a plus, not a minus.

Why? Because an employer's flexibility is perfect for you. Your pitches can influence the employer to your advantage. A company's unstructured approach to hiring and lack of rigidity can sometimes enable you to capture your dream position. Laurie did. If the university had required years of high-level management experience for their new dean, they would have eliminated Laurie immediately. Instead, they interviewed her and allowed her to overcome that objection. That's what the right pitch can do. Now let me introduce someone I'm going to call Ned Hepner, an expert in doing things *his* way. He is the same person I told you about in the previous chapter. **Now in his seventies, a highly successful financial entrepreneur working and exercising daily, Ned comes onto our stage and reflects back on his career, beginning in his twenties.**

"You know? I always wanted to ask you something. How do guys like you make a living?"

The three of us, my cousin Audrey, her engineering-student friend Jack, and I, were sitting in her living room in Cambridge, and Jack had just asked me that question. Audrey was a senior in college, and I was just completing my master's program in French literature. Everyone else in the French master's program was going to teach, and I had no such ambition. I studied French simply because I loved the language and the literature. It would be silly, wouldn't it, with a master's degree in hand, to continue with the doctoral program if I didn't want to teach? Of course it would be silly, and wasteful. I would just have to get a job. There was no choice, really, because the scholarship money would stop if I didn't remain in school.

I began looking for work in June, the same week that school ended. Understand that I was a true liberal arts type. I never took a course in economics, business law, accounting, finance, or a similar marketable skill. There was little, in fact, that I had to offer a prospective employer other than, what? My love for language? My love of literature? The employment agency people were not very impressed.

So I looked. And they looked. The weeks passed, until one day I saw want ads for a dictionary editor at a major New York publisher and a college sales representative for a textbook publisher in New England. I responded to both ads and received an offer, for the same money, from each publishing house. There was nothing to the college sales-rep job, for which I interviewed first. They hired me in twenty minutes. I spoke the language, looked the part, had the degrees, and could drive.

The interview at the New York publisher was another story altogether. They needed someone who could write, and with experience, preferably in writing and editing dictionary definitions. All I could show them was a master's essay about a sixteenth-century French poet. And I certainly had no work experience, except for five summers as a soda jerk at Howard Johnson's and two years as an export clerk for a textile broker during my graduate years. No help there. The interviewer was just about to dismiss me when I asked him a question. "I use dictionaries," I said. "There is more to dictionaries than just definitions. There are words, after all, with pronunciation keys and etymologies. I know the phonetic alphabet. And, listen please. Because Latin, the root of all Romance languages, was a prerequisite for my master's degree, I have a working knowledge not only of French but also of Spanish, Italian, and Romanian. I know how each of these languages evolved from the Latin. Furthermore, I have also studied German, Hebrew, and Aramaic. Don't you think that I could add something to the etymology effort? That I could help, too, with pronunciations and syllabifications?"

I was a hired as a pronunciation editor. Within three years I was a senior editor of the dictionary, fully responsible for half of the definitions in the new unabridged edition, as well as the choice of new word entries. Twenty-two editors reported to me, and I was in line to be the managing editor of the next college edition.

During my third year at the publishing company, I got married, and my wife became pregnant shortly afterwards. "New York is no place to raise a child," she said. "What do you think about moving to California?"

"Look, dear," I replied. "I'm a Bostonian New Yorker who's never been west of New York or farther south than Philadelphia. Not only do I barely know where California is, but I've never even been on an airplane." (I was twenty-eight years old at the time). "Well," she said, "if we don't do it now, we'll never do it. With the dictionary almost done, you'll be starting on a new project and we'll be trapped. Look, we've got nothing to lose. If California doesn't work, it doesn't work. We can always come back. And my friends tell me that San Francisco—that's where we're going, by the way—is just like Boston. It even has a bay!"

This was crazy. San Francisco, my foot. But I decided, for a little peace, to humor the wife and send out my résumé to a number of employment agencies in San Francisco. What a response! They said that, in addition to a number of magazine publishers and university presses in the area, there were numerous book-publishing houses in San Francisco. With my background and experience, they would have no problem placing me.

I left my publishing position in April and flew to San Francisco. My wife would follow after I got a job. Appointments with several employment agencies were already set for the day after I arrived. Given that we did not have much money, I arranged to stay in an inexpensive hotel in a section called the Tenderloin, which, I was told, was within walking distance of the downtown business district. I figured that it would take a week, maybe two, to find a job based on what the employment agency folk reported.

Uh huh. The Tenderloin turned out to be the red-light section of San Francisco, populated largely by prostitutes and the homeless. The hotel was inexpensive, no question, but with good reason, as I quickly found out. Well, no problem. I would only be there for a short time.

Uh huh. The short time turned out to be seven weeks. San Francisco is a small town. It is not New York. There were more editors on my staff at the publishing company than in all of the publishing houses in San Francisco. And the editors, all of a certain age, were not leaving any time soon. I was advised to sell shoes in the interim. Moreover, unlike most other small towns, there was a tremendous inflow of new immigrants to the San Francisco Bay Area, all of whom, it seemed, were looking for work at the same time and in the same places that I was. The magazines. The university presses. The newspapers. Trade periodicals. House organs of major corporations. Equally distressing was the fact, also new to me, that San Francisco was basically a branch-office town. True enough that most of the national companies had offices here, but the offices, typically, were small and with few professional employees.

Okay. Four weeks had passed. It was plain that I was not going to find an editing job there in the foreseeable future. The few opportunities that seemed to be available were in F.I.R.E. (Finance, Insurance, and Real Estate). So I took myself to the library to use the typewriters and changed my résumé. I would now be looking for a management trainee job instead of work as a senior editor. The new résumé, I told the employment agencies, should be circulated among the banks, insurance companies, and real estate brokers. And so they did, but they continued their editorial search as well. There was little or no hope, they said, that a F.I.R.E. company would hire a twenty-eight-year-old management trainee with no business background, training, or experience regardless of how many words he knew and how well he could spell.

Uh huh. But they were wrong. Eventually. Three banks responded to my résumé the first week it was on the street. The first two responses, as it turned out, were generated simply by curiosity. What was a big-time editor from New York doing in San Francisco looking for a trainee job? The only answer that made sense was that I would only be biding my time at the job, until I found one more suited to my education and experience. Then good-bye. Thanks, but no thanks. We should have known better than to ask you up for an interview. Sorry we wasted your time. And ours. The third bank was different, in the sense that I kept being passed from each doubtful interviewer to the next. "No" was the simple, and perhaps even the correct, answer. But instead, everyone with whom I spoke seemed determined to find out how, if at all possible, they could find a way to hire this fellow.

It was week six. I was in the municipal bond department of the bank. Last stop, I was told. If not here, then the effort would be over. The night before the interview, I went to the library to find out what the devil were municipal bonds. And oh, by the way, what was a bond? Turned out that municipal bonds are IOUs (bonds) issued by state and local governments to finance their construction, operational, and program needs. These IOUs, which typically run from one to twenty years, are sold by banks and brokerage houses to individuals as well as insurance companies and other institutional investors and repaid with interest over the life of the IOU. Great, I thought, I have a lot to offer here. As I waited for the interviewer in the outer office of the bond department, I was reminded of a story my father told me years ago. He was walking in the street one day when he bumped into an old friend. Nice coat you have there, my father said. His friend laughed. Heck, Harry, I'd give you the coat but it's too big, won't fit. My father answered, "Coat like that? I'd make it fit!"

The interviewer and I sat down in his office. He didn't have much time, he said. It's obvious that you're not qualified for an administrative, sales, or trading job in this department, so those positions are out. We do have an opening in the research section, but that job requires, among other things, that you have a thorough knowledge of California and some real technical skills. I'm sorry, but . . .

Research people write, don't they? I asked. "Yes, we publish circulars about the bonds we're selling, which describe the governmental units issuing the bonds, their economic profile, and the security pledged for repayment. There's one right on my desk. Now, if you'll excuse me . . ."

I picked up the circular. Skimmed it, and said, "Wait, please." I took a pen from my pocket and, as he looked over my shoulder, I began editing the document. Within two minutes I found three typos, and five misspellings, and I restructured two incomprehensible sentences. "Should I continue?" I asked. He sat down. Do you publish anything else, like area brochures or general sales documents? Do people here make speeches? "I'd like you to talk to my boss," the interviewer said.

The bank hired me in week seven, after I spoke to the interviewer's boss and three other titled heads. And yes, I did make the job fit. I worked for the bank for twenty-two years, moving from a research associate in the bond department to a senior vice president of the bank and a national authority on municipal finance. In my first years, I took night courses in economics, accounting, and banking at the University of California Extension as well as computer technology at UC Berkeley. I wrote speeches for the division head and ultimately for the president of the bank. Time passed and my career moved forward. Instead of taking courses I was now giving them, as a guest lecturer on taxation, government, and securities issues in colleges and graduate schools of business. In addition to my departmental responsibilities for the bank, I was serving as a director on a variety of internal bank boards and special committees. My opinions on banking and finance were sought by trade papers and the national press. I had, in a word, arrived.

What did Ned do to match himself to a position that he had *never* held, in an industry in which he had *never* worked? Let's look at his strategy at the publishing company. He didn't focus on the position for which the publisher was interviewing—someone who could write, preferably with experience in writing and editing dictionary definitions. (Why did they interview him at all? Remember, the employer's lack of clarity is your best friend.) Instead, he focused on another skill set—pronunciation—which he possessed, clearly and precisely articulating those skills in relation to the publishing of dictionaries.

Ned framed his questions to articulate his fit with the creation of the dictionary.

The Result:

Ned sold his brand. The publisher hired him as a pronunciation editor, even though he never had worked as a pronunciation editor or at a publishing company.

Ned, in his twenties, had already mastered the power of the pitch.

What did Ned really do?

He used what I call the Pick, Probe, and Pitch broadcast. The combination of the three Ps varies according to the situation. Let's look closely at how Ned employed the broadcast at the publishing company.

Pick: Select the focus of the broadcast—Ned selected pronunciation and related aspects.

Probe: Ask questions to obtain information and/or show the fit—Ned asked questions to show the fit.

Pitch: Probe to Pitch or Pitch to Probe—Ned did both to articulate and match his skill set to the dictionary.

In interviewing for the banking position, for which he was not qualified, Ned used the three Ps again, varying his technique.

Pick: Ned selected "writing" as the focus of his broadcast.

Probe: Ned began the broadcast with a probing question: "Research people write, don't they?"

Pitch: Ned edited a bank circular in front of the interviewer, finding mistakes as a way to demonstrate his skills. He created a nonverbal pitch, which, in that case, was a demonstration. Don't assume that the pitch must be verbal!

Ned then probed again to assess the impact of the editing—his nonverbal pitch—on the interviewer. When the interviewer sat down, he responded affirmatively to Ned's question, "Should I continue?" And Ned continued his broadcast to demonstrate the fit.

The Result:
Ned sold his brand again. The bank hired him as a research associate, even though he had never worked in this capacity or at a bank.

I hope you noted that Ned did something above and beyond making his outstanding broadcasts. He Managed the Process. In both situations, the interviewers were ready to say good-bye when Ned took charge of the interview and began broadcasting. In both situations, the employers hired Ned to perform different functions from those that had prompted the interviews. At the beginning of his career, Ned learned how to use the broadcast to Manage the Process to achieve his goal.

(Entrepreneurs: In cultivating clients, you too should use the three Ps' broadcast. Your goal is to convince potential clients to "buy" your products or services. To do that, you must broadcast your fit to show the match, as Ned did. If you do not match and you cannot fix the fit, then don't pursue the client who is the wrong fit.)

Divergent and Convergent Thinking:
The Keys to the Kingdom

I learned the significance of divergent and convergent thinking abilities, the foundation for my three Ps' broadcast, while writing my doctoral dissertation on creativity. Here is how I learned that divergent thinking requires analysis, and convergent thinking requires synthesis of information.

Assessing two distinct approaches to identifying creativity, I studied a group of screenwriters who were completing their master's degrees in the theater arts department at UCLA. To explain it simply, I examined personality, on the one hand, incorporating attitudes, interests, and values. And, on the other hand, I looked at the so-called cognitive-factor approach that emphasizes the intellectual aspects of creativity. I selected tests to evaluate both approaches. The students' writing professors rated their creativity according to the standards I created.

I met with each screenwriter individually and administered the tests, never disclosing that I was studying creativity. I had a wonderful time collecting my data, until I met Colin Higgins. For his master's thesis, Colin wrote *Harold and Maude*, which was turned into a movie that's become a classic, followed by *Silver Streak* and *Foul Play*. With Shirley MacLaine, Colin co-wrote *Out On a Limb*. He directed the movies *Nine to Five* and *The Best Little Whorehouse in Texas*.

When I met with Colin, his quiet determination struck me. He had no problem completing the tests until I gave him the divergent thinking tests, which required him to respond very fast—completing each in just two, three, or four minutes. Colin froze. His face turned beet red. He simply could not list uses for common objects such as a shoe, watch, key, and safety pin in the time allotted. I didn't know what to do. I was concerned about his intensity and didn't want him to see himself as a failure. Ultimately, he put down a few responses and finished the tests. I reassured him that his performance was fine, and it was. To be creative, many people need to have time to incubate ideas, and the amount of time varies widely among individuals.

My point is that in designing your broadcast you need to formulate questions that require the employer to think divergently. You are probing for information. It's up to you to ask the right questions to gather the key information you need in order to demonstrate your fit. If you feel as if you are "pulling teeth" to elicit the information, so be it. Some people are naturally forthcoming; others are not. If the person pauses to think, don't assume that he or she is not forthcoming. It's certainly easier to interact with people who readily tell you what you need to know, but be sure to wait patiently for a response and give the person plenty of time to think.

Remember, divergent thinking requires analysis. Convergent thinking, on the other hand, requires the respondent to synthesize information. Here are some examples of questions that elicit both divergent and convergent thinking:

Divergent-Thinking
Questions to Ask the Employer

- In the next five years, what new direction will your company take to generate more revenue?
- In the next year, what are the benchmarks of achievement you envisioned for this position?
- What are the growth opportunities for my skill sets in your company?

Convergent-Thinking
Questions to Ask the Employer

- Ideally, by what date do you want to fill this position?

- How many direct reports would I have?
- Is this a new position or are you refilling the position?

In your hand, you hold the *keys to the kingdom. Your* ability to frame both divergent- and convergent-thinking questions the Right Fit Way is crucial to mastering the broadcast, and those questions are the keys. The answers to your questions provide the information you need to demonstrate the fit.

When and Why to Broadcast

Let's return for a moment to your résumé. I know you're eager to send it, but we haven't completed it because your goal in the Right Fit Method is to demonstrate an exquisite match between you and the employer—and your written, verbal, and nonverbal broadcasts must be tailored to show that fit.

Before the Interview

You wrote your résumé to fit a specific position for which you hoped to be given an interview. Now that you've arranged that interview, it's time to finalize the résumé to fit the position perfectly. You may think this is a bit backward, but it isn't. You can't determine the extent to which you are the Right Fit until you obtain as much information as you can from the employer. Even if you're a 100 percent match for the position, you still need to call the employer to pitch yourself and arrange the interview. If you send the résumé *without* calling, it is highly likely to be lost in the sea of résumés the employer receives. You must differentiate yourself from others by displaying your brand. And to do so, you must call the employer.

If the position description or posting does not state to whom the new hire will be reporting, you'll need to do some sleuthing. This will require divergent thinking—brainstorming. Let's consider a few ideas. Check the company's website for the name or names of key people; call the department that houses the position; or call the human resources department. In a large company, call the CEO's assistant, who will have the answer or find it for you quickly. If the company operator requires you to name someone in order to transfer your call, select a name from the company's website and ask for that person in order to make some progress. If all else fails, order the annual report and continue sleuthing with that. Note that you must think divergently to achieve your goal and continue to do so until you succeed. In the Right Fit world, there's no frustration, only winning!

I hope by now you have found the names and information you need and are ready to begin cold calling. Strange as it may seem, I love cold calling. I really do. I view it as a search and discovery mission. Cultivating your own curiosity is key to your success. Curiosity prompts questions, and questions can elicit valuable information.

If you have little or no curiosity, it's difficult to question naturally, which is an organic process that requires strategy. *As Ned showed us, it's a verbal tennis match, requiring listening intently and responding with lightning speed, without focusing on competing against someone.* I can't give you a list of questions to use as a template, but I can give you a proven approach to use, as well as provide you with techniques such as divergent and convergent questioning.

The Cold Call

If you have difficulty making a cold call, you are probably focusing on yourself and your fears, and not on the task. Instead, focus on the task, and forget about rejection. If you do as I suggest, you should have no problem cold calling. You will be proud of yourself for changing your behavior, particularly if cold calling has been difficult for you in the past. Let's begin perfecting the art of the pitch.

Preparing

First determine whether you have a one- or two-step process. If you can *immediately* call the employer to whom you would report, this is a one-step process. If you have to speak with an assistant to find whom that person is, you have a two-step process ahead of you. Sometimes, you may need to speak with more than one assistant, requiring still more steps. That's why I recommend calling the assistant of the head of the company, who either knows the answer or can tell you how to get it. Regardless of how many steps you face, lay all the contact information you currently have on your desk. Now you're ready to prepare your pitch or pitches, keeping in mind that you need to be fast on your feet.

Pitching to Proceed: How to Pitch to an Assistant

The goal of this pitch is twofold: to obtain the name of the employer to whom you want to speak and to establish rapport in case you need to call back. Let's begin with rapport, which is your "prelude." Introduce yourself and say something that is friendly and courteous, focusing on the person to whom you are speaking. Here's an example:

"I'm Michael Ralston, calling from Chicago. I hope you're having a great day. We're experiencing a terrible snowstorm here. How's your weather?" If you are calling a warm-climate zone, laugh and say, **"You're lucky. You never have to worry about snow."** The point is to treat this person as a human being, not a voice. Visualize a person and create an icebreaker to establish rapport. You need to feel comfortable with your icebreaker message. Then, ask a question to elicit the name of the person you want to reach. If you have the title, give the title. If you do not have the title, then create a statement to communicate that person's specs. For example:

"I'm trying to locate the person who heads the _____

department. Can you give me that person's name and direct line?"

The person with whom you're speaking may say you will need to speak with that person's assistant and will give you that phone number. That's fine. You then call that assistant and either arrange a time to speak with the employer or, as a second option, ask to be transferred to the employer or his or her voice-mail. You will need to decide, based on how well you establish rapport, which way to go. If the assistant asks you the purpose of your call, which is standard procedure, your pitch should be directed at *needing information.* You must say something *requiring* the employer's level of expertise in order to avoid being transferred to someone else. If you are not successful in arranging the appointment or transferring directly to the employer, then leave a voice-mail pitch for the employer and for the person in human resources who is handling the search, if that is appropriate. Concurrent voice-mails are fine, but be sure the message is consistent.

The bottom line is that you need to obtain more information to determine whether you are the Right Fit for the position. If you are, then of course you want to arrange the in-person interview, complete your résumé incorporating the "new" Right Fit information that matches more key points, and send the résumé to the employer prior to the interview. If you determine through Picking, Probing, and Pitching that you are the wrong fit, then do a "Ned" to determine whether you fit another position at the same company. You don't want to waste your time or the employer's. If there's a match, proceed. *If not, simply say to yourself, "Next!" Close that door and open another. No suffering or fretting.*

You're probably saying, "But I don't know exactly what to say when I'm speaking with the employer on the phone or how to handle my voice-mail message." I haven't given you the "ingredients" of the pitch yet because I want to tell you more about how to Manage the Process. Let's start with the voice-mail message. Your broadcast must be compelling enough to elicit a call-back from the employer or human resources department. To achieve that, it's important to write and practice the pitch, until you sound natural, not "canned" like a telemarketer.

Ingredients of the Voice-Mail Pitch

Tone: Upbeat, fast-paced, warm, strong voice creating a visual image of moving quickly.

Body of the Message: Succinct and to the point, without extraneous information. Here's an example:

"I'm Michael Ralston, calling from Chicago about the Director of Auditing opportunity, for which I am ready. I match your requirements. I am a Big 4 CPA, audit manager, traveling 50 percent, specializing in HMOs, with ten years of auditing experience."

Note the specificity of the message in showing the match. No vagueness. It is businesslike and to the point, making it clear that you are ready to be promoted, if this is a promotion opportunity. You want to motivate the recipient of the message to call you to find out more. If it appears to be a lateral move because the level of the position is similar, then say something about more responsibility or the geographical location, selecting what is appropriate and true.

Closing the Message

Include your precise contact information. State your mobile phone number and/or personal e-mail address only. If you are unemployed and you must leave your home phone number, be certain that the voice-mail message on that number is your voice and references only you. Be sure to suggest times that you are available to speak and try to arrange a phone appointment, which is the ideal. In concluding your voice-mail message you can say, "I would like to arrange a time to speak with you." Then, give your availability. On call-backs, be sure to answer the phone yourself. If you cannot answer the call, then your voice-mail should pick up the message. Remember, you are closing the message and closing the person concurrently.

   Following Up: If the person does not call back, then follow up until you speak with that person, unless you discover that the search has ended for whatever reason—the position has been filled or the search canceled. You may feel like a bit of a pest in following up, but it is necessary.

Ingredients of the Telephone Pitch

   If you are speaking on the telephone after having left an initial voice-mail message, be sure to reiterate your fit again so that the interviewer can probe. Remember, this is a telephone *interview*, even though it may not be labeled as such. Pay attention to your tone. Let the verbal tennis match begin. Listen carefully. Then ask divergent-thinking questions to expand your understanding of the position. They are evaluating you, but—equally important—you are evaluating them. The fit must be the Right Fit for you and for them. For example, if you are now traveling 50 percent of the time and want to be sure that travel will not suddenly consume 75 percent of your time, ask a divergent-thinking question: "Could you describe the travel schedule, including the cities?" Then, you continue probing until you find out what you need to know. Do not ask a convergent-thinking question: "What is the amount of time I would be traveling?" You'll get a percentage. It's up to you to carefully delineate what you need to know and ask the "right" questions to elicit the responses you need to determine whether to proceed. Pick, Probe, and Pitch to achieve your goal, proceeding to the next interview, if the position is the Right Fit for both of you. Do *not* arrange an in-person interview if you are firmly convinced the opportunity is the wrong fit, unless you want to learn more about the company to identify the Right Fit at that company, at which time you must broadcast, as Ned did.

If you are unable to arrange an in-person or subsequent telephone interview without sending your résumé first, you need to continue working on your pitching ability. *The ideal is to arrange the next interview at the end of the conversation and then send the résumé, which you manicured to show the fit.*

Mastering the telephone broadcast takes time and practice. I recommend that you do role-playing with a friend or significant other to practice the techniques I have outlined. Again, Pick, Probe, and Pitch, using appropriate tone coupled with speed and content. As you practice, first play the role of the candidate. Then, after you master it, play the interviewer so you can experience that role as well. Having a good sense of what the employer will say can be of significant help to you during your actual telephone and in-person interviews.

Pitching in Person

Let's take stock. You have written the Right Fit résumé for a specific opportunity, mastering one type of written pitch. Then you "aced" the telephone interview, mastering the verbal telephone pitch, with or without the voice-mail message. Now, your big moment is here. You've reached your in-person interview. You'll need all your pitching skills, including those that are nonverbal. Remember how Ned observed his interviewers rising from their chairs to leave and began pitching again. Prepare, prepare, prepare.

And remember the photographic artist Doyle? Here's his pitch:

When trying to get published, I first sent a selection of my photographs to a greeting card company in Colorado. A month later, the photos came back in the mail with a letter from the art director saying they could not use my images. I then called a company in Northern California, and they gave me an appointment to show my photographs in person. At the beginning of my appointment, the art director told me she would look through my portfolio and pull out some images that she liked, and later show them to the company president. She said he was too busy to look at all of my images. She started pulling out pictures, and soon was pulling out every other print.

Before long, the president entered and the images were presented to him. After viewing them all, he turned to me and said, "These are very good. Do you have any more?"

The art director looked at me in amazement because of the president's apparently uncharacteristic response. I smiled and gave him my portfolio.

He pulled out many more pictures and added them to the pile his art director had created. He then told me he was interested in publishing my photographs, *if* I could convince him that they would sell as note cards and posters.

I had noticed when entering the outer office that the company's entire staff was women of various ages, and women are the principal buyers of note cards and posters. So, I proposed a demonstration: "Let's select twenty of my images and lay them out on the desk. Then invite your office staff in to view them. I guarantee that you will hear at least four different comments from the staff: The younger women will say, 'These images are beautiful. Could you photograph me?' The mothers will say, 'Could you photograph my children?' The grandmothers will say, 'Could you photograph my grandchildren?' And the rest will say, 'I wish you could have photographed me at that age!'"

The president agreed at once. The office staff entered and viewed the images. Many "oohs" and "aahs" were heard, and then, one by one, each of my predicted phrases was uttered. After the fourth statement, the president laughed and asked the group, "Should we publish them?" The office staff answered with a resounding, "Yes!"

Remember the first company I submitted to, in Colorado? About six months after my note cards were published,

I happened to see a catalog for that company. They had come out with a series of note cards with images similar to mine, but not exactly in my style—photographed by the art director who had turned me down!

What did Doyle do to elicit an offer? The following:

- He arranged an in-person interview to show his photographs rather than sending them. He had experienced firsthand that sending the photographs led to no interview but resulted in the art director imitating his work. Sending information to an employer that includes photographs, résumés, or other material without "setting the stage" with a verbal pitch does not enable you to share your brand quickly or learn more about the employer and the position that can help you prepare for your in-person interview. Sometimes, you might be lucky and get an interview with only minimal information in hand, but most often, you will lose an opportunity for the interview because you failed to pitch yourself on the phone.

- He observed at the interview site that the entire staff in the office was "women of various ages" who "were the principal buyers of note cards and posters." He planted the seed of this image in his mind to incubate.

- He brought an extensive portfolio from which he selected photographs and then gave the entire portfolio to the art director when asked to do so. Note that he mentioned "smiling" at the art director—a nonverbal acknowledgment indicating he would be delighted to show more photographs.

■ He immediately presented an effective verbal pitch, which, in that particular case, was a demonstration in response to the president's request. He remembered the "women of various ages" and predicted how they would respond to his photographs. Doyle proposed involving the women to show that he understood the "Right Fit" buyer. All the women's "predicted phrases were uttered" and he won the position.

Doyle's broadcast was flawless. Think about Doyle's approach to determine which aspects of the pitch are applicable to your situation from a conceptual perspective. Creating pitches prior to interviews and during interviews is challenging, requiring a quick "reading" of the person or persons with whom you're speaking.

Mastering the broadcast takes time. Reread Ned's and Doyle's stories to better understand and experience their techniques. Review and practice the basic strategies and approaches I've outlined until you're ready to "road test" your broadcast. To master Managing the Process, you need to broadcast your pitch confidently. Have you seen the descending ball at Times Square on New Year's Eve? Remember the excitement it elicits? You will experience a similar amazing adrenaline rush immediately after a successful pitch leads to an offer. Are you ready now or will you soon be ready to broadcast? If so, then

YOU ARE

Trigger Tip
Visualize the
Packaged to Pitch logo

Put on your mitt and let's go!

CHAPTER EIGHT

Sharing Your Brand: Manage the Process

Your Goal:
Take Charge!

Managing Your Career

NOTHING IS MORE IMPORTANT to your career success than actively taking charge. Let's explore what that means. *You* are responsible for your own outcomes—positive and negative—not anyone else. Even if you have experienced career pain, such as unexpected downsizing, *you* must respond in ways that work to your ultimate benefit. Too many people spend lots of time steeping themselves in self-pity, which prevents them from managing the process to their own advantage. Complaining about a current situation or an unfortunate circumstance only distracts you from focusing on what to do to get what you want. I know two brothers who work in the same professional field; they are equally talented and capable. For decades, one brother has complained about the myriad ways in which he believes his parents were unfair to him. This brother has achieved moderate career success. The other brother forgot long ago about his parents' shortcomings during their childhood. He was nominated for a Nobel Prize.

If you stay focused on your goals, eliminating every distraction, you will soar to heights you never dreamed possible. Patti Rager achieved extraordinary career success, and so can you. Patti enters the spotlight now and tells her story in her own words:

> I always wanted to become a registered nurse. As a young girl, I excelled in science, and it has always fascinated me. As I grew up, I tagged along with my parents, both of whom were business people who volunteered for numerous good causes. I learned the value of service and giving back from my parents. So, the combination of science and caring for others made the nursing profession a natural choice.
>
> After I finished college at the Medical College of Virginia (MCV) in Richmond, I landed a year-long nursing internship at their medical center. This internship gave me a solid foundation during the critical first year of my professional life. I had a mentor who encouraged me at the center where I received clinical-skills training, participated in group debriefing sessions, and was socialized into the profession. I worked with patients in several of the areas in the center, which gave me breadth of experience through clinical rotations in different specialties. After the internship, it was time to leave the nest. I worked as a clinical nurse on a busy surgical unit, in critical care, and on a pediatric unit. I was on a "high" as I gained more clinical skills and got a taste of making a big difference in people's lives and their health. I thrived on the "emotional paycheck" I received from my professional relationships with the patients, and I vowed I'd never do anything else.

That is, until I was offered a nurse manager position on a pediatric unit at a Catholic community hospital. I admired the nursing director, and although I was inexperienced at age twenty-four, she saw something in me and encouraged me to take the new role. When I told her I was intrigued but that I loved taking care of my patients, she said, "You can influence more patients' care by leading staff members who will, in turn, care for their patients in the best possible way." She was right, and I've seen it over and over in my career: happy, talented, engaged employees make for happy patients/customers and better outcomes for the business.

As a nurse manager, I worked hard with my staff to develop new programs such as parent support groups, preoperative preparation parties for children, and recreation therapy, which were all innovative concepts at the time. I wanted to learn more about the science of pediatric nursing and refine my managerial skills, so I began a master's degree program in nursing management part time at night while I was working full time. I read as many books on management as I could find, and immersed myself in budgets, quality assurance, and human resource issues.

I particularly enjoyed having nursing students visit my hospital unit. They were always inquisitive and excited to be working with our patients. One day, their nursing professor approached me about a faculty position at my alma mater. I remembered my nursing director's words about my influence on patient care as a leader when the professor reminded me of the important role faculty members play in shaping the skills of future nurses who will care for many generations of patients over the course of their careers. And, in the end, I was swayed by the offer to teach pediatric nursing and nursing leadership, my two areas of particular interest. I was comfortable with the faculty at MCV, after all, many of whom had taught me as a young nursing student. They took me under their wings, and I soon realized how much you learn when you teach! I didn't realize it then, but this faculty experience would serve me well when my husband was later transferred to Philadelphia, where I worked in the College of Nursing at Villanova University. Later, I established an internal nursing newsletter called "Nursing Notes," which became an informal and fun communication tool for our staff in a Texas hospital.

When my husband was transferred once again, this time to Boston, I was fortunate enough to land a position at Massachusetts General Hospital. I was in awe of the quality of the people who worked there and of the patients who came there from all over the world. I needed more challenge, so I developed a "Spend a Day with a Nurse" program in which employees in all departments—maintenance workers, pharmacy techs, and physicians, even board members—spent shifts with registered nurses at patients' bedsides. The program gave everyone a sense of how important nurses' roles are to patient care, and it gave the nursing staff a big boost of confidence and sense of appreciation. It was fun, informative, and created "buzz," as did the magazine *Caring*, which I launched with a colleague and our creative team.

Eventually, my boss asked me to direct a merger of our hospital business units and the nursing units throughout all of our hospitals, creating a new division in the Massachusetts General system. I moved budget responsibility from the business managers to our nurse managers so that financial decisions would be made by those who oversee patient care. The new division interfaced with every department in the hospital. We were able to identify impediments to excellence in patient care, and make improvements on an individual and systemwide basis.

I loved this job because we were able to make big changes by everyone working together. We became the "hub" of communication and change. I was a member of the Nursing Executive Committee, but my leadership group members were all non-nurses, many of whom had MBAs, and I soon realized I wanted to go back to school for my own MBA to hone my skills in finance and operations.

About this time, my husband was promoted to a new position in New York City, and I ultimately received an executive nurse fellowship from the Commonwealth Fund Foundation that allowed me to study for my MBA at Fordham University, and I was allied with an important network of nurse-executive colleagues from across the country.

While I was studying finance, accounting, economics, and business strategy, I constantly pictured myself working in a medical center, armed with my newfound skills. I visualized myself in hospital budget committee meetings, skillfully pleading my case on behalf of my patients and staff. But I couldn't yet foresee how much my process-improvement, marketing, and advertising courses would help me in my *next* unexpected career move.

Patti continued to climb up the career ladder, rung by rung, managing the process all the way. Her next decision would change her life more dramatically than any decision she had made before. Carefully note Patti's passion as she took this new leap, confident in her talents, her skills, and her instincts. I hope you're discovering that your career fuel is the same as Patti's— passion—and that it can carry you farther than you ever dreamed.

My husband and I had moved again—this time to Washington, D.C.—when I began to search for a nurse-executive position, but the first call I received was from Kevin Smyth, a publishing entrepreneur. He wanted me to interview for a position as executive director of a company called Nursing Spectrum, which would entail launching a new magazine for nurses, also called *Nursing Spectrum*, and managing an office in the Northern Virginia area. At first, I thought I wasn't interested because my heart and soul were in clinical and administrative nursing, and all of my goals and education were geared exclusively toward nursing. Then, I remembered how much I'd enjoyed my public relations and newsletter projects through the years. I decided to take the plunge and learn more, and was soon interviewing with Kevin in Chicago. The Chicago edition of the magazine was being produced that day, and I had a chance to see the editorial, production, and sales staff in action. The scene reminded me of the old "Mary Tyler Moore Show" as they worked quite happily, it seemed, at a frantic pace as their deadline loomed. The magazine they were producing was all about registered nurses and their careers, and I was quickly bitten by the publishing bug!

I was deep in thought during the plane ride home. I must have been fidgeting, because the young man sitting next to me asked if there was something wrong. I replied, "No, but I just met a man who's turned my life around 180 degrees." He smiled and said, "Isn't love great?" I laughed and assured him that I was happily married and hadn't just fallen in love.

When I got home, I was eager to discuss the exciting new possibility with my husband. This unusual opportunity would allow me to communicate with tens of thousands of nurses every two weeks, and I could combine my nursing and business skills on behalf of the nursing profession. We would highlight local nurses' stories, and finance the magazine with RN employment advertising. I would put my MBA to use right away. It was a chance to start my own business with someone else's money, and my boss would be halfway across the country! My husband gave me his whole-hearted vote of confidence, and I accepted Kevin's offer, agreeing, almost impossibly, to begin the next day. (Did I mention that this all began in my kitchen?) Yes, it was a big career risk, but my intuition told me this was a big chance that was worth taking. I might never get this opportunity again, and I'd always enjoyed starting new things.

I worked feverishly, immersing myself in editing techniques, cover photography, layout and design, and consultative selling. I attended night classes on publishing at Georgetown University, and networked with nurses and their employers at every opportunity. I established a small office and hired a small, but creative and committed, staff. We believed we could do anything—and we did. We produced a beautiful magazine in just under six weeks, and the nurse readers and advertisers loved us. We celebrated for about fifteen minutes; then we raced to get ready for our next deadline, just two weeks away.

Any entrepreneurial adventure takes passion, hard work, long hours, and creativity. Technical glitches, snowstorms, and other small calamities didn't faze us. We immersed ourselves in everything about nursing to find the best stories and creative photography and to make our sales goals to keep the magazine afloat. We all believed in what we were doing together, and this fueled our success. Soon, Kevin asked me to launch another magazine in Philadelphia, and it, too, was a big success. Next, we launched our first website—which was very new territory in 1997. And today, after sixteen years, we have fourteen magazines, three websites, a thriving continuing education business, television programs, and a growing direct-mail business. We also host forty-two career fairs each year.

Along the way, *Nursing Spectrum*—our original magazine—was sold to Gannett Company, Inc., a Fortune 500 company, which is probably best known as the publisher of *USA Today*, the nation's largest newspaper. Subsequent to the sale, we acquired NurseWeek, a company based in San Jose, California, that was similar to Nursing Spectrum, giving us the largest reach of any nursing publisher, circulating our products and services to more than one million registered nurses and nursing students.

When Kevin left the company, I replaced him as president and publisher not only because I felt an obligation to our executive team and staff members, but also because I had ideas for new product launches and services that I'd been wanting to introduce. Such ideas included updating our magazine production and circulation technology, honing our editorial and consultative-selling skills, and conducting regular customer-service training for all employees. We eventually hired twenty-eight registered nurses in important roles throughout the company and increased our staff to 170 people. Our goal is to reach more nurses, more ways, more often, and we pride ourselves on creativity and responsiveness.

My past sixteen years in publishing have been a remarkable ride. I'm thankful that I took the plunge because my work is extremely rewarding. I believe I have the best of both worlds in my "hybrid" career—one foot very much in the rewarding nursing field and one foot in the exciting publishing world, where I became chairman of my company. Publishing, like nursing, is demanding work, with numerous deadlines and details. I joke that critical care nursing prepared me for the chaos and heart-pounding moments of our early press days. I didn't realize it at the time, but I was practicing for my publishing role when I took on writing projects throughout my nursing career. My take-away lessons from my career are:

- Always remember your roots. My passion for publishing is directly tied to communicating with our nurse readers.
- Don't be afraid to take calculated risks.
- Work like mad!
- Remember, it's all about the people. You must focus on your employees daily. Nothing happens unless they are as devoted to your mission as you are.

Patti Rager, RN, MSN, MBA
Former Chairman, Nursing Spectrum

I hope the story of Patti's career journey—from hospital nurse to chairman of Nursing Spectrum—inspires and empowers you. I was struck by Patti's passion, commitment, and academic achievements. She continued to learn what she needed to know in order to succeed, building a toolbox filled with knowledge and skills that enabled her to reach the top of nursing publishing. As you may remember, Jason, Doyle, and Ned also kept learning in order to become number one. They and Patti are excellent models for employees and entrepreneurs to emulate: actively pursuing learning to advance their careers.

Now, let's distill Patti's career decisions and actions over the years into their key components:

- Consistently and repeatedly, she managed the process—continuing to climb the career ladder as she moved to different regions of the country to accommodate her husband's career.
- Changed her behavior immediately—an essential ingredient for managing the process—including her willingness to begin her new position at Nursing Spectrum the day after she accepted it.
- Fueled her career with passion for nursing as the foundation, consistently expanding and changing the function of her Core Identity.
- Continued to learn and grow—welcoming the suggestions of others whom she respects and pursuing advanced degrees and courses to "fit" her career changes.
- Acknowledged mentors who helped her build her career.
- Exuded confidence, coupled with an engaging, positive, upbeat attitude, approaching the

world as filled with new opportunities she couldn't wait to manage, building on all she learned along the way.
■ Valued her employees.

Time after time, Patti shared her Personal Brand with employers to capture the "Right Fit" positions. *She competed with herself, never against others.* She appreciated and acted on mentoring advice in order to grow. She recognized that she had to continue to educate herself in order to succeed in the new opportunities she accepted. She incorporated all she learned as she built Nursing Spectrum, an entrepreneurial adventure. Patti Rager is now a "name brand" in the world of nursing publications. Remember Patti as you build your career. Manage the Process to achieve your goals, welcoming new opportunities as stepping stones to success.

Managing the In-Person Interview

In chapter seven, I demonstrated how to pitch yourself on the telephone, implementing a key strategy in managing the process. I hope that by now you have had a terrific telephone interview and are preparing for the in-person. Depending on the employer, you may have many "visits," and in every interaction you must Manage the Process consistently, never making any assumptions, including the details of your compensation package. If you are the Right Fit candidate for the position, you will believe yourself to have magical powers as you Manage the Process the Right Fit Way.

I once placed a physicist, whom I will call David Doran, in a high-level management position. Prior to David's interview, I carefully instructed him *not* to discuss salary issues. I always instruct my client-employers similarly, making sure they do not discuss compensation with the candidate or candidates they interview. Sometimes, when my client-employers "love a candidate," it's difficult for them to follow my request. But if they want me to capture the Right Fit candidate for them, it's very important for me to do the "closing," not them. And to guarantee the best result, I ask candidates to honor my request as well, telling them exactly what to say to prospective employers to help ward off the salary discussion.

I thoroughly enjoy managing the process with both employers and candidates, which includes debriefing them following interviews. **When I debriefed David, I heard something that will be engraved in my memory forever. I think of him as "The Imprisoned Candidate." David is entering stage right. Please enjoy this exciting story in his own words:**

> We were driving through the streets of what was, to me, an unfamiliar city, and with every passing block it increasingly seemed that I was trapped in a scene from Sartre's *No Exit*. The driver, a middle-aged woman, was chatting incessantly as she drove us to a restaurant that would serve as the site of my interview. Petunia was the company's human resources vice president and, because I was captive, she figured she'd buffalo me as we drove.
>
> Mercifully, we'd be dining with others as well, including the head of the search committee, who had interviewed me over the phone a few weeks before. Famous in his own field, and on the way to becoming even more renowned, Carey had apparently chosen the restaurant. Several other people would be there as well, diluting Petunia's dinnertime repartee.
>
> But for now, *Petunia had me trapped in her car, and she was relentlessly talking at me.* The conversation finally turned to salary, and how much I was looking for. Arlene Barro had prepared me for this moment, so I was armed

with a righteous feeling of immunity from Petunia's expectation that I should fess up and cough out a figure. Arlene had told me—as she also had told Petunia and others—that I was not to discuss salary. Arlene would take care of that. Pause now for a flashback: Arlene calling me to discuss this new position in a faraway city, Arlene convincing me that I should seriously consider this position although the idea of moving from my exciting East Coast city to that distant location seemed odd, to put it most politely. But, in the end, I had agreed to be presented for the position by Arlene at what was indeed a renowned institution, and I had put myself in Arlene's capable hands.

She told me the field of candidates was quite small. She had tracked me down and, after perusing my résumé, was convinced that I was the right fit for the job. I found it odd that I wasn't in contention with two dozen other candidates for this particular job. It seemed too easy. Or so I thought until Arlene went to work with me. Arlene grilled me about myself and my career and went about guiding, encouraging, and mentoring me as I rewrote my résumé to match the blueprint she had created for the position, based on what she had elicited from the employer. And while that sounds like a contrived way to try to impress a potential employer, it wasn't. My résumé—my education and life and professional experiences—did, in fact, match what the employer was looking for. The only really hard thing for me to do was re-write my résumé so it rang like a giant biographic bell to make the employer love that song and communicate the message that they couldn't afford *not* to hire me.

I looked over my new résumé. "I did all that?" I asked myself. Yup. I guess I was quite the terrific candidate, at least according to the blueprint—and the revised résumé— that Arlene had coaxed out of me. No wonder there weren't other candidates. But the rest was up to me.

So, after the first day of interviews with movers and shakers at the institution, here I was with Petunia as she grilled me about my salary demands. I told her Arlene had made it clear that I was not to discuss this matter; and that no one was to ask me about it. Incredibly, Petunia simply restated her question: "How much are you looking for?" I repeated my Arlene mantra, thinking that would make Petunia feel uncomfortable for having pushed the issue. But no, to my disbelief, Petunia asked the question again, only louder this time. "HOW MUCH ARE YOU LOOKING FOR?" She asked me at least three times, in fact. And she was insistent enough that I felt both uncomfortable and irritated.

Yet I knew from my experience to date with Arlene that the smartest thing I could do was to follow her advice. Arlene would take care of it for me. She would do the negotiating this time. And I would learn from my experience with her how to negotiate when I found myself in such a situation in the future. Whether I was more angry than uncomfortable in that car with Petunia I can't recall. But I do know that Petunia finally got tired of trying to pry out of me something that I had no intention of giving her. A figure.

Finally, we reached our destination. During dinner, Carey mentioned to me that they normally take only those candidates they really want to hire to that particular restaurant. I was surprised at how brazenly he had laid his cards on the table. But grateful. So, I reciprocated and told him I really wanted the job.

In the end, I not only got that position, but I got it with a great salary and a sign-on bonus that let me buy several great pieces of furniture, including the wonderful maple dining room table I'm sitting at as I write this story. New furniture is not a trivial issue for me, either. After years of dragging vintage hand-me-downs from city to city, I bought new furniture for my new home by a lake.

And I now enjoy more financial security than I ever had before. It's a new life. And that's what Arlene does: She changes lives. She not only changed my life, she armed me with the savvy and confidence I need to put my feet down confidently on the next rung of my career ladder, whenever that will be. *Arlene taught me to fit myself into a position, not compete for it.* And on the day when I take that next step up the professional ladder, I'll say hello to my future and good-bye to Petunia.

In his humorous style, David does a wonderful job of describing his frustration with Petunia, and how he never gave in to her questions about salary. Yet he made it very clear to her, Carey, and the others at the dinner interview that he wanted the position, something I had told him was very important to do. If a search consultant is representing you, it's critical for you to let that person negotiate the terms of your offer. In chapter twelve, I will explain how to manage your interaction with a search consultant to get the package you want and how to manage the employer yourself to do the same.

I shared David's story to demonstrate the importance of managing the process during an interview. If David had disclosed what he wanted as a salary, I would not have been able to negotiate an optimal compensation package. The winning candidate must become a master strategist, managing the process with attention to the "devil's details."

Master These Effective Strategies

During the entire interview period, you must consistently Manage the Process. Master the following behaviors. Practice them through role-playing so you can implement these behaviors comfortably, naturally, and automatically.

- Articulate that you are the "Right Fit" clearly and concisely, point by point.

- Assert yourself confidently, saying what needs to be said without waiting to be asked a specific question. It is your responsibility to broadcast the fact that you are the "Right Fit." It is not the employer's job to figure out how to elicit the information from you.

- Anticipate objections. Use Pick, Probe, and Pitch to overcome all potential employer objections to hiring you. If you learn, for example, that your start date needs to occur within a short time frame, figure out how to do this and reassure the employer of your flexibility.

- Create divergent-and-convergent-thinking questions that you are ready to ask, selecting the stage of the interview process when it is best to pose them. For example, discussing your relocation package during the first telephone interview is premature. Remember Ned? He is the master of timing, a key component in "closing."

- Say what needs to be said and no more. Do not provide extraneous information, especially about your personal life. The employer does not need to know, for example, that you have been married three times.

- Repeat key points to reassure the employer, alleviating specific concerns, such as your ability to finish a degree or obtain a particular license or certification by a targeted date.

- Thinking and responding fast is essential. You must anticipate the unexpected, changing your behavior effortlessly and graciously. For example, if you arrive at the interview and the

CEO's assistant tells you that there was an emergency board meeting and your interview needs to be rescheduled, use the opportunity to get acquainted with the assistant, rescheduling with a smile on your face.

■ Answering all appropriate questions is vital. But answering inappropriate questions is not necessary. You need to decide what an inappropriate question is for you. Then, you respond with grace and tact. Think about it before the interview begins.

When you have mastered the effective behaviors that I have outlined, you can take charge of the interview, managing the process effortlessly and sharing your brand successfully.

Trigger Tip
Strategize to take charge of the interview

Let's hop to it!

CHAPTER NINE

The Calculated Close: Finish the Deal Before It's Done

Your Goal:
Close yourself first, and then close, close, close!

CLOSING BEGINS and ends with you. Before you can successfully close a deal with someone else, you need to learn how to close yourself—personally first, and then professionally. To become a superb closer, you need to master both the personal and professional, managing the process with the right pitches.

Closing Yourself on a Personal Level

Focus is a key component in closing a deal. And it's very difficult to maintain a laser-like focus and exude self-confidence if you are unhappy with yourself. That's why we need to help you identify and eliminate your internal cobwebs before we go further.

A woman in her forties, whom I will call Sabrina—a Beverly Hills homegrown beauty—is someone I've known for a long time. For many years, she had been an executive assistant to the president of a huge public relations firm, but then suddenly she found herself unemployed, the details of which I will share in chapter thirteen. Following her downsizing, Sabrina took a long break to help her get her bearings again, and then she began searching for a new position. After many months without success, and having become increasingly tired of searching, Sabrina experienced an epiphany: She had to work on herself first.

She felt "like a salmon swimming upstream," she explained to me, and desperately wanted to change. First, she made sure she got out of the house every day, shopping for fresh foods after she had exercised at the gym. Then, she began networking and attending social events. Before long, Sabrina had lost fifty-eight pounds. Feeling great about how she now looked, she decided to take the *worst* job that she could get in order to motivate herself to find a really good position. She wanted to feel so desperate in an awful job, she told me, that she would find a way to get out. For Sabrina, the worst job she could find was telemarketing, which she did from 1:00 p.m. to 10:00 p.m. daily. She said, "I threw myself into a 'ditch' [her telemarketing job], and after four weeks I left the 'ditch.' My strategy had succeeded. I was ready to move ahead."

Start working on those cobwebs now so that they do not interfere with your professional life. For Sabrina, facing the fact that she needed to take off weight was very important. From her perspective, the weight was an impediment to her career success. She then needed to dig herself a "ditch." Sabrina's strategy worked, and she was ready to begin her search for the Right Fit position, feeling motivated and in charge of herself. What do *you* need to change about yourself?

Closing Yourself on a Professional Level

Before you start searching for a new position, it's vitally important for you to determine the parameters of your Right Fit position, something you have already done in chapter five. There, you created the Blended Blueprint, which I would like you to review and revise, as necessary. Perhaps you could not relocate earlier, but events in either your personal and/or professional life may have made that possible now. Throughout your life, it's essential to re-evaluate current circumstances, adjusting to them as necessary. For example, relocating babies or small children is easy. The parents are in charge. But as children turn into teenagers, that's another story. Recognize and act on life events in ways that benefit you. Sometimes we forget the freedoms we have, turning down opportunities that could be ours if we were open to them. If Patti Rager had not agreed to start her new position at Nursing Spectrum the day after her interview, using her "unpacked" kitchen as her first office, she would not have become the chairman. Go for it!

Calculating the Close to Capture a New Position

Total focus is absolutely necessary in order to close successfully. What does that mean? Now that you have closed yourself personally and professionally, you are ready to focus all your attention on "calculating the close to capture a new position." Step by step, detail by detail, from the first contact with the employer and forever more, you are closing. Even after you start your new position, you must continue closing. But for now, let's focus on how to close the deal.

Many candidates, as well as employers, see closing as the final step of the interview process. It's not. The candidate must close every step of the way to ensure that the employer makes an acceptable offer. The employer must constantly close to be sure that the Right Fit candidate will accept the offer that is extended. All too often the deal falls apart at the end because both sides have held their cards too close to the vest, so to speak. It's far better to determine early in the interview process whether the deal can be done. If the final negotiation is not possible, determine this in the early stages of interaction with the employer. Don't waste your time and the employer's.

Let's walk through the steps that are necessary in order to close the employer. First, coordinate your ability to pitch and Manage the Process so that they work together as a team. You must naturally Manage the Process, pitching as you go and keeping in mind your desired outcomes. Think back to when you first learned how to drive a car. Initially, you had to think about each task—turning on the ignition, putting the car in gear, and so on. After a while, the several processes became automatic. Driving to your destination is analogous to closing the deal.

References

When you are actively searching for a new position, it's very important to inform your references of the positions for which you are being interviewed. Ideally, the employer will give you advance notice that your references will be checked. If the "new" supervisor happens to know one of your references, it's very easy to pick up the phone and call. That's why it's essential to keep your references well informed so that they are prepared for every eventuality. If, for example, you identify objections during the interview process that need to be overcome such as "your limited management experience," be sure to discuss this or other objections with your references.

Stellar references are powerful closing tools. You are not pitching yourself; those other people who know you well are pitching you. These broadcasts must be very strong, reinforcing your Personal Brand to close the employer. If the employer harbors doubts and is considering interviewing other candidates, stellar references will help remove that doubt and eliminate the need to see more candidates. The employer will be highly motivated to hire you and be more open to negotiation. Strong references, especially those from high-caliber people, often significantly enhance the terms of your offer. Maintain an ongoing relationship with your references, keeping them updated on your accomplishments. You never know when you may need them.

I wish I could share with you the detailed references of the candidates I have placed in my search practice. Some of them are truly exquisite. But, in order to maintain the confidentiality of my client-employers and candidates, I cannot. I can, however, quote from these references to demonstrate the caliber of those candidates, which has had a significant positive impact on my ability to close their Right Fit deals for them. References become even more important when you are representing yourself, because you do not have an intermediary—like a search consultant—to speak for you. (In chapter twelve, I'll show you how to apply the Right Fit Method when you work with a search consultant.)

From an employer's perspective, the purpose of checking references is twofold: one, to confirm that you are who you purport to be and two, to determine whether you are the Right Fit for the position at hand. In all of my search career, only three times have I had to recommend to my client-employers not to hire candidates based on their references, and each time, it was because the candidates were not who they had purported to be. The first candidate falsified his expenses on travel vouchers; the second lied about her accomplishments on her résumé; and the third took credit for work that her employees had done without her involvement. One reference for the latter candidate said, "She drinks coffee. I don't know what she does." This candidate lost the opportunity to take a vice president position because of that shockingly poor reference. Be aware of the impressions that you make on all the people you come in contact with in your work environment. You never know who says what to whom and how it may affect your career success. Be aware!

For an employer to determine whether you are the Right Fit for a position, it's important to ask questions about your personal attributes, interpersonal skills, and technical capabilities. Let me demonstrate, from real references, the kinds of statements that truly impress employers, confirming the Right Fit and the candidate's credibility.

As a search consultant, I must put my client-employer first. In reference checking, I try to find out very quickly if the candidate has serious flaws. Recently, I conducted a search for a vice president of public relations. I created a blueprint for the Right Fit candidate, recognizing that I was searching for a rare bird—in this case, a PhD scientist with superb interpersonal skills who had a strong public relations background coupled with superior writing skills. There were additional specs that made the search nearly impossible. Undaunted, I proceeded and found a candidate, whom I'll call Jonathan. He not only met my client's expectations, but exceeded them— *setting a standard against which no one could compete.*

When I checked Jonathan's references, this is what I learned. In response to the question, "Would you re-employ Jonathan if you had a suitable opening?" One reference responded, "I tried to rehire Jonathan on several occasions, but I could not afford him. I would hire him again in a heartbeat!" Another of Jonathan's references said, "We've tried to rehire him because he has endeared himself to us. We see him as part of the inner circle of our group. He makes things work. We treasure what Jonathan did and does." If Jonathan had serious flaws, he would not have received strong endorsements to rehire. And if that had been the case, I would have probed to find out why.

If any employer you have worked for would not want to rehire you, it's very important for you to explain the situation to the "next" employer, so the call to that reference doesn't produce a surprise. Cover all the bases! Prevent problems before they occur. Obviously, it's sometimes a bit tricky when a "next" employer calls your current employer for a reference. If you already have informed your supervisor that you are looking, then it's not an issue. But if your supervisor does not know, you must prepare him or her for the impending call. If you are not comfortable doing this for whatever reason, don't do it. Trust your instincts!

The strength of your relationship with your supervisor is likely to be a key factor in determining how that person will respond when asked to describe your skills. If you have built a solid relationship, your supervisor's response should be encouraging and supportive, and he or she should be "sorry to lose you." If, on the other hand, your relationship with your supervisor is not as strong as it could be, create the right pitch to enlist that person's support. If this approach does not work, select someone else in the same organization who knows you well enough to show how you fit the position for which you are being interviewed. But be sure that the employer will accept a substitute for the direct supervisor, before enlisting that person as a reference.

Some states have laws that govern what employer references can say about you. Keep in mind that because a search firm is not an employer, such firms can access more information to share with client-employers than the employers themselves can obtain. Chatting off the record to obtain information about candidates is also a commonplace way to gather information.

By the time I had checked all of Jonathan's references, a clear picture of his stellar attributes had emerged. According to his several references, Jonathan was:

". . . a person you like to be in the presence of. He has a chemistry that is hard to define. Because of his chemistry, he knows more about us than anyone else. We schmooze."

". . . a hard worker and not a clock watcher. He also has a high threshold under pressure. He has no outbursts under stress."

". . . a pleasure to work with. He had a certain spark that lit the place up."

". . . so committed that he continues to think about my needs and e-mails information to me [after leaving]."

". . . a great guy and a joy to work with. If you asked him to do something, you did not have to worry about it. He is a 'can do' guy."

". . . someone who asks the right questions . . . very loyal . . . composed, with a sense of humor, which makes him a natural leader among his peers."

". . . has the requisite skills and intelligence to comprehend complex scientific matters and translate that into materials that the lay audience can not only understand but also appreciate."

". . . knows how to distill information . . . can portray the scientists' messages in a way that makes people proud."

"Jonathan's scientific judgment was superb. He had a very good understanding of the nuances of science and the nuts and bolts. He took the arcane and the highly complex and translated it. Most scientists write as scientists. Jonathan did not do this. He had the ability to translate very difficult scientific information into easily understandable language for the press. He writes very well."

My favorite quote about Jonathan:

". . . exquisitely sensitive to press deadlines . . . could recognize hot buttons . . . knew how to juggle simultaneously, while still observing priorities . . . had the nose for news . . . never eaten alive by the press . . . always knew where the landmines were."

Jonathan's references confirmed that he was not only the Right Fit for the open position but also the Total Package—the flawless fit. He lacked nothing. His references confirmed that he performed at a standard against which no one else could compete. The result: I presented an enticing offer to him, and he accepted.

There's no substitute for stellar references. Those broadcasts confirming that you are who you purport to be and are the Right Fit for your "next" position are invaluable to closing the deal.

(Entrepreneurs: Determine how to incorporate the benefits or results of your services or products in closing new clients or customers. For example, Tom Lombardo's foreword to *Win Without Competing!* is an excellent illustration of a client's written testimony. Think about your business and figure out what needs to be said about you and your products and services, what satisfied clients you can quote, and/or what data you can use to support your claims. Use the information when you pitch—whether verbally or in writing—to broadcast your Personal Brand or name brand.)

Your Big Day

On the day of your first interview, as well as all subsequent interviews with the same employer, it is very important to keep this mantra in mind:

> I don't know who the decision makers are. I cannot assume anything. I will interact with everyone I meet in a courteous, friendly, respectful manner. I will present a single, consistent image of who I am. Even if something irritates me, I will keep a smile on my face.

The Interview Begins Now

Enforce your mantra with the building guard and every assistant you meet in hallways, elevators, and restrooms; *enforce your mantra.* An inadvertent negative comment from anyone could kill the deal. On a big day early in my career, when I interviewed for a position at the National Cancer Institute, I had to wait four hours to meet with the division director, who was delayed by an emergency. I used the opportunity to become further acquainted with the people with whom I would be working. By the time I met with the division director, the deal was almost done.

While you are enforcing your mantra, you must pay careful attention to the pace at which you are walking. It's crucial to walk *briskly,* exuding the aura of self-confidence coupled with high energy. A fast-paced walk communicates an important message to the employer—this candidate looks like someone who can get the job done.

Let the Tennis Match Begin

At each interview, focus on closing, which means communicating your Personal Brand *consistently*: Manage the Process to pitch why you're the Right Fit for the position. Pick, Probe, and Pitch using divergent- and convergent-thinking questions to elicit more information about the opportunity in order to match . . . match . . . match to close . . . close . . . and close. The stronger the match, the stronger the close. During the interview process, don't think about how you feel about what you're hearing. If you do, you will start focusing on yourself and forget to Manage the Process. After you ace the interview or interviews, think about what you've learned. Review your Blended Blueprint to help determine whether the opportunity is the Right Fit. You do not want to accept an offer for a position that is not perfect for you. Too many people do this and are very sorry later.

How to Finish the Deal Before It's Done

Implementing the strategy of the Calculated Close enables you to finish the deal before it's done. You wonder, *Why does this really matter? Why can't I discuss the total employment package at the end?* This step-by-step closing strategy is necessary because you don't want to:

- Waste your time if you can't ultimately close. Early on, you need to determine the employer's flexibility in relation to your needs.
- Haggle at the negotiation stage, because this may negatively impact your relationship with the employer. The gradual close ruffles no feathers.

Present the package to your family or significant others to help determine whether you have omitted key elements or that the position is not the Right Fit. Concurrently closing your family and your new employer will eliminate the unexpected from either side, which could affect the closing of the deal.

Memorize!
The Creed of the Calculated Closer:
Make No Assumptions.

Visualize yourself at the interview, ready and eager to close gradually, and always in control. You Manage the Process effortlessly, using Pick, Probe, and Pitch, asking divergent- and convergent-thinking questions. Your focus is entirely on closing—broadcasting your exquisite Right Fit. Think of nothing else. Focus, focus, focus.

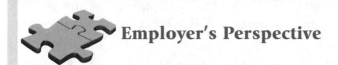 **Employer's Perspective**

The employer wants to hire someone to fill a specific position. If the position is ongoing and no changes have been made, then the employer is replacing a previously filled position. If the process (the tasks that should be performed) or outcome (the achievements) for that position have been modified, it is a quasi-new position. But if a new position has been established, you may be playing in a different ballgame. The specs of the Right Fit may or may not be clear to the employer. In theory, the more the employer knows about the position from past experience, the easier it is to identify the Right Fit. But that isn't always the case. If the person who formerly held the position was the wrong fit, then the position is much like a new position. In this case, the employer is still trying to determine the Right Fit.

It is crucial early on in the interview process to determine the status of the position for which you are being interviewed. If you are being considered to refill a position that was previously held by the wrong fit, probe to find out why the company hired the wrong fit. The goal of the probe is to figure out whether the employer has a blueprint of the Right Fit, even if the wrong fit was hired along the way. Probe to elicit the specs of the blueprint. Those are the specs to which you will match yourself. If the position is new, probe to determine the specs of the blueprint, keeping in mind that you are looking for employer flexibility. It's important to have enough information to create the match, but some flexibility is also extremely valuable in helping you shape the employer's expectations to select your Personal Brand.

For example, let's say that the employer wants you to have experience in managing fifty or seventy-five people, but you've only managed twenty to date. Let's look at how a candidate of mine named Susan handled this problem. This was what her former employer, one of Susan's references, had to say about her:

". . . Susan was viewed by management as a director who had growth potential in our organization. She had it all: CPA, MBA, and Deloitte & Touche. She performed at a high level and was effective. We viewed her as being able to assume other high level positions."

". . . Susan's responsibilities grew quickly in less than a four-year period. In her first position, she supervised about ten people. When she left, she was supervising between seventy-five and a hundred people."

Susan specifically asked her former employer to discuss her growth and the number of people she had supervised over a four-year period. He cited the number of people Susan had managed to show that she was ready to grow more.

Because the new position required more responsibility, at her interview Susan pitched how she had grown, discussing her effective management style and broadcasting that she was ready to manage 140 people as the company's new vice president of finance. She carefully probed to be sure that the key managers who would report to her were in place. Susan didn't want to promise what she couldn't deliver. By asking questions that showed she knew what she needed in order to succeed, she convinced the employer that she could perform well.

Susan was fortunate. Her new employer could clearly articulate the Right Fit. But that's not always the situation, as I've said.

When you prepare to meet with an array of interviewers, check to be sure that the key decision makers agree about the specs of the position. Different viewpoints are common. It is obviously easier if there's agreement, but if not, you will need to direct everyone's focus to weighting the specs. Each spec can't be equally weighted, so it's up to you to elicit from the interviewers what specs are most important to them, then to reinforce your fit to their highest weighted specs first, and subsequently to the others.

By the end of all your interviews, it's important for you to have reconciled disparate viewpoints about what specs constitute the Right Fit, as well as to have demonstrated to the employer or employers that you are indeed the Right Fit. If you have succeeded, the major portion of the Calculated Close is completed. The rest is duck soup! Chauffeur yourself toward the conclusion of the close slowly and deliberately, without missing any turns in the road. Here's how.

Listen carefully for "buy signals," which are usually questions or implied questions. Respond consistently to all interviewers, without indecision. (If you receive no buy signals, assume nothing. Perhaps more internal discussion among the interviewers needs to take place before they reach a decision.) Here are some examples of employer buy signals:

When can you start? In response, ask the employer to indicate the desired start date. Match it as closely as you can. If you need to give more notice to your current employer than the "next" employer's proposed start date would allow, find a compromise. Be sure to say something like, "I would like to give a month's notice to my current employer. We have an excellent relationship, which I would like to maintain."

What salary do you have in mind? Tell the employer why you want the position, and reiterate what you will achieve and how you fit the organization. Then ask the employer to tell you what the company has in mind. Don't simply ask about salary; find out what you can about the whole package they are offering. If the employer quotes a lower figure than you had anticipated, it's up to you to cleverly change the offer by incorporating other elements. Use your divergent-thinking abilities to suggest options to broaden the elements or perks of the offer. Salary is far from the whole deal. Here are *some* examples of elements to consider incorporating into the structure of your offer:

- Raise salary in six months
- Sign-on bonus to enhance the relocation package
- Performance bonus based on mutually agreed upon outcomes
- Commission, if applicable
- Stock options, if applicable

Let's think even more divergently:

- Office location, size, and decor
- Assistant, shared or unshared
- Assigned or unassigned parking space, paid by employer

The level of the position influences the number and kind of perks you can negotiate. For example, if you have budgetary responsibility and hiring authority, you may have specific needs in these areas. And you may be able to negotiate additional vacation time, depending on how the benefits are structured.

The list is virtually unlimited when it comes to what can be negotiated. Remember not to make the assumption that you have to be a high-level manager to receive any or most of the perks I listed. It's up to you to ask for what you want, including severance, in the event of unexpected downsizing. Just be sure that the employer views your requests as reasonable. There's a fine line you must be sure not to cross. Be careful not to ask for too much, such as college tuition for your children. If you do, the employer might suddenly begin to see you as difficult to please, and you could lose the position just as you are about to get it. That's why it's important to close as many elements as you can throughout the interview process, not waiting until the official offer stage. The gradual close will be less painful for you *and* the employer.

What are your relocation needs? Ask the employer to tell you the company's policy on relocation. Prior to the final interview, you should obtain quotes from three different moving companies so you can tell the employer how much it will cost to move you. Obtain the quotes with and without the mover packing your belongings, including the option for unpacking. If you have a fragile item to move, such as a work of art, find out the cost of moving that item as well.

Temporary housing, short-term storage, and house-hunting trips are all elements in the relocation realm, each of which you can and should discuss. Depending on the employer, there are usually some opportunities for negotiation. You will need to probe to figure out the parameters for those discussions.

All companies have policies governing compensation, benefits, and relocation, some more flexible than others. In my experience, it's not the policies that prevent the deal from closing, but the interaction between the negotiators. If you Manage the Process the Right Fit Way, you should be able to close, provided that you *are* the Right Fit and ideally the "flawless fit," the focus of the next chapter.

Expert closing requires practice. Be sure to complete the role-playing scenarios I outline below. Thinking fast on your feet is essential to expert closing. Use the role-playing exercises to train yourself to think faster. Ask a friend or significant other to play three different roles: assistant, supervisor, and human resources professional. Review "Master These Effective

Strategies," which I articulated in chapter eight, before you begin role-playing. Then, practice those behaviors during your role-playing.

Role-playing before your big day could make the difference between closing and not!

Here are the scenarios:

Assistant

The protocol in this instance is that you need to interact with an assistant to arrange your first in-person interview with your "next" supervisor. The assistant makes it difficult for you, suggesting dates and times that are impossible for you to meet. The assistant, quite imaginative, will create an array of stumbling blocks. In turn, you must be gracious in order to get what you want, turning the assistant into your advocate. If you interact with the assistant the Right Fit Way, managing the process and pitching to achieve your desired outcomes, you will arrange the interview, and the assistant will become your ally. That assistant could make the difference between your being offered a position or not.

Supervisor

You must convince the supervisor that you are the Right Fit. To do so, it's important to practice interacting with a supervisor who says very little. This supervisor sits back and lets you probe and pitch to show that you're the Right Fit. As you do, the supervisor should become more communicative. When that happens, gently probe to determine whether the position is a refill, quasi-new, or new. Use this information to continue closing, gently probing for information on the whole compensation package, including the array of perks I outlined.

Human Resources Professional

You must convince the human resources professional that you are the Right Fit. That person is probably working hard to find your flaws to reduce the possibility of hiring someone who is the wrong fit. You must overcome any objections thrown at you, such as the fact that you have changed positions frequently, or that you have too little or too much experience. After you overcome these objections, then you can probe for information about benefits. Be gracious in your probing.

Good luck in role-playing!

Trigger Tip
Stay cool, calm, and collected, constantly closing consistently

Let's shoot for the stars!

CHAPTER TEN

The Total Package:
The Flawless Fit

Your Goal:
Discern and dwell on the devil's details.

The List Is Endless

TRUST ME ON THIS: Employers pay incredibly close attention to a candidate's flaws. They listen intently to what a candidate says, and they carefully study behavior and appearance. Employers evaluate the significance of a candidate's flaws and determine whether it's in their best interests to proceed to the offer stage. It's crucial for you to understand what employers see as flaws so you don't present them. And in some instances, you will need to create a pitch to overcome the flaw or flaws that you cannot conceal. What's particularly challenging is that it's virtually impossible for you to determine the weight the employer will give to the flaws you have—weighting that can vary dramatically among employers. Let me share some stories from my search practice that highlight candidate flaws and the different ways in which employers and candidates tend to perceive them.

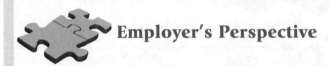 **Employer's Perspective**

Early in my search career, I had a CEO client-employer who was immaculately groomed. He was a living magazine cover. He came to my office to conduct a particular interview and asked me to sit in. Knowing that presenting the proper appearance was essential from this fellow's perspective, I was even more focused than usual on the candidate's appearance as I prepped him for the interview, and, from my perspective, the candidate had it all. As the interview got underway, I watched the tennis match unfold between my client and the candidate, a young man in his late twenties. The verbal exchange was going well, but then I observed my client staring at the candidate's leg. His legs were crossed, exposing part of a bare, hairy leg. His too-short socks were bunched around his ankles, and I'll never forget the sight. Nor will I forget that this was an egregious flaw, which that particular employer simply could not forgive. The candidate did not get the job, and from that day to this, I always discuss with my male candidates the need to wear long socks.

You may think the employer overreacted. Perhaps he did, but the point is that the flaw, which was preventable, distracted the employer from interacting with the candidate effectively. You do not want that to happen to you!

On another occasion, I had dinner with a very promising candidate the night before her interview. She had everything my client-employer valued for the Right Fit.

Together, we reviewed every detail of what she planned to wear to the interview. My only concern was her ability to maintain a laser-like focus during the interview, because she confided that she and her significant other were having difficulties.

When I later debriefed my client-employer, I learned that my candidate had come to her interview with a button missing from her suit. "There are no excuses for missing buttons," he said. I knew that her personal life had distracted her, and, of course, the missing button had distracted him. Please don't lose the opportunity for an offer over a missing button!

Another time, I was reviewing the key components of my flawless Right Fit Method with a candidate on the evening before her interview. We discussed, or so I thought, precisely what she would wear. When I called my CEO client-employer to debrief her, I reached her executive assistant first, and she began to laugh. "Dr. Barro," she told me, still quite amused, "she wasn't dressed like the other candidates you have sent us for other positions." "She wore a lovely suit, didn't she?" I asked. "That's correct," the executive assistant responded, "but over her lovely suit she wore a leopard-skin cape." I paused and said a bit incredulously, "A leopard-skin cape?" She responded, "Yes," and started laughing uproariously again.

Interestingly enough, those who interviewed her, including the CEO, were not distracted by the leopard-skin cape at all. In fact, they found this aspect of her Personal Brand—her flair for clothes—appealing. Shortly thereafter, I extended their offer to the candidate, whom they couldn't wait to hire. Yet you can be assured that the other two employers I've mentioned would have viewed the leopard-skin cape as a minus, not a plus. And that's why it's not always a simple matter to become the flawless fit.

Habits

When I debriefed still another client-employer following an interview, the reviews from more than a dozen company interviewers were glowing. Everyone loved him, but there *was* one concern. As the candidate spoke, he continually put his hands on his face and moved them in different directions, and the employer asked if I could speak to the candidate about this. I decided that first I would observe this behavior over dinner, at which time I certainly saw what my client had pointed out. But, in the end, I concluded that "silence is golden." Why? Eliminating short socks, sunglasses perched on top of the head, missing buttons, and leopard-skin capes are easy changes to make. But habits are *not* easy to change. I was concerned that if I discussed his hands-on-face habit with the candidate, I would make him self-conscious, which might negatively impact his delightful personality. It was only after the candidate had accepted an enticing offer, but before he started the new position, that I chose to discuss his habit with him.

Think about habits you have that could negatively affect "closing the deal." For example, direct eye contact is necessary to convey truthfulness and honesty. Employers are *keenly* aware of eye contact—or its absence. They will almost always evaluate whether you look directly into their eyes. When you practice the role-playing scenarios I outlined in the last chapter, ask the person who is role-playing with you to observe your eye contact behavior and to see if you have other habits, such as shaking your knees, that need to be changed. Find your own flaws first, and correct them before your big day.

Physical Imperfections: Structure and Function

I define structure as those elements that constitute your physical appearance, including weight, teeth, and hair. Function includes walking, lifting, sitting, and standing—the ways in which you move. Our society focuses on structure. Consider the billions of advertising dollars that are spent to help us look better. And employers are keenly aware of structure, too.

While I was coaching a candidate for her interview, I mentioned the importance of exuding warmth, using smiling as one important technique. She told me she could only smile with her lips closed. "Why is that?" I asked. "Because I have no front teeth," she explained. I probed further and learned that she had a hereditary problem that had required her to have her teeth pulled, and that, after a year-long search, she had found the right dentist to replace her teeth. I thought, well, that's good news, but what should I say to my client-employer before the interview? I decided to say nothing.

When I debriefed the client-employer after the interview, his first question was, "Do you know that the candidate has no front teeth?" I said, "Yes, I do." Then, I explained the situation. It turned out that the company's major concern was, in fact, the candidate's teeth. I explained that within two weeks, the candidate would have a lovely set of new teeth, and we delayed the next interview until after that time, so the candidate could demonstrate her beautiful smile. And soon thereafter, I presented the candidate with a great offer.

If you have a visible structural situation that you are in the process of fixing, it's important to be honest with the employer. Otherwise, you may be "dismissed," never knowing the reason why. Remember, it's always your responsibility to say what needs to be said.

Lifting is an important function for some professional positions. Nurses and physical therapists, for example, need to be able to lift their patients. But does a nurse who is a faculty member at a college need to be able to lift patients?

Once, while I was conducting a search for a nursing professor at a college, I found a dynamic candidate who had seriously injured her shoulder lifting a patient, and who had made the decision to move from working in a hospital to academic nursing. Before her interview, we discussed her lifting restriction and hoped it wouldn't be a problem. She loved nursing, had academic experience, and very much wanted the position for which she was being interviewed. On her big day, a panel of interviewers from the college directly asked the candidate whether she could lift a patient to demonstrate to students how to do it. She explained her injury and subsequent limitation, suggesting that it could be readily overcome if someone else lifted the patient while she verbally described the procedure to the students. But the panel of interviewers simply responded that lifting was a *requirement* of the position. They wouldn't budge. The candidate was very disappointed and felt she was treated unfairly. Other academic institutions might have responded differently to this candidate's physical limitation, and, of course, she ultimately found a teaching position for which she was the Right Fit. If you have a physical limitation, don't give up! Continue searching for *your* Right Fit position.

You may be asking yourself: "Why can't I be just the Right Fit? Why do I have to be the *flawless* fit?" The answer is that an employer who observes a flaw may use it as an impetus to probe for other imperfections, unraveling your Right Fit Personal Brand in the process. Sure, you will be able to overcome some objections to your flaw or flaws. But it's better to prevent objections in the first place, which is the basis for the flawless fit concept. Never forget that you are the ultimate decision maker. If an employer's standards are not the Right Fit for you and there's no flexibility, it's up to you to decide whether you want to accept a position with that employer. Be honest with yourself. Do not accept a position you know is the wrong fit.

Preparing for the Big Day

Stand in front of a full-length mirror. Ask yourself: "What needs to be fixed?" I'm not talking about losing twenty pounds overnight. Instead, I'm simply asking this: "Do you look well groomed?" Examine your appearance from head to toe, paying particular attention to your hair, face, hands, and fingernails. Whatever needs attention, you must correct and adjust before the big day. To help guide you in the grooming process, determine a specific image you want to project. For example, if you want to project a mature image, keep in mind that coloring and styling hair does wonders for both men and women. Remember Susan, the candidate for the vice president of finance? My client-employer didn't like her long, flowing hair because it made her look too young.

With regard to your face, it's very important to convey the sense that you are approachable. I had a candidate who looked unfinished because half of each eyebrow was missing. All she needed to do was extend and shape her eyebrows, which she did. If your eyebrows are bushy, you may need to trim them.

Several issues will influence the extent to which you use makeup—the industry, the type of position within that industry for which you are being interviewed, and the particular employer. I suggest that women wear at least some makeup to enhance their features and warm up their faces. Women who wear no makeup remind me of unmade beds. They look unfinished. If you're a woman who doesn't like wearing makeup, or you don't know how to apply makeup, go to a makeup artist and learn how to do it. It's not the amount of makeup that you use that's important, but rather the effect the makeup has on your appearance.

An energetic, healthy-looking face is an asset for both women and men. And men need to pay as much attention to this fact as women. For example, moisturizing your skin could soften the lines in your face, as it does for women. Think about what else you could do to enhance your face. If you have a beard, determine whether you should trim it or remove it.

Hands sometimes show signs of aging. Again, moisturizing your hands is important. When you shake the employer's hand—firmly but never in a death-grip—the texture of your skin should not be rough. You want to communicate your self-confidence with the strength of your hand, not the roughness of your skin, something that could easily distract from successfully communicating your message of self-confidence.

Your fingernails should enhance your hands. It's very important for your nails to be well-groomed, and their length should be appropriate to your profession. For example, can you envision a surgeon, gynecologist, or dentist with long nails? Clear nail polish is fine for both women and men. If you are a woman and want to use a color, select one that is not a distracter—like the leopard-skin cape.

What Should I Wear?

This is an age-old question, and the answer is simple. Dress in a way that communicates that you are the Right Fit for the position. No distracters! When you arrive for your big day, the chatter begins. But the only buzz you want to start immediately is that you are well-dressed, and look presentable and professional in every way. Even if the culture of the company is informal, remember that you are there for a formal interview. If you have spoken with the employer on the telephone prior to the interview—which I hope you have done or soon will do—feel free to ask whether you should be dressed in business-casual or in a suit. For the purpose of the interview, business-casual for men should be interpreted to include a sportcoat, tie, and slacks. Women should wear separates, either jacket and pants or skirt. There are exceptions to this definition of business-casual, of course, depending on the industry. Be sure you know what is appropriate dress for an interview in your industry.

I strongly suggest wearing closed, polished shoes (no spike heels for women) and hosiery. Men, remember that your socks should be long enough not to reveal your legs. Women should wear long hose if they are wearing pants, or natural or matching hose if wearing a skirt. Bare legs and bare feet are almost always distracters, although, even in this case, there could be industry-based exceptions.

Colors exude warmth, especially pink, orange, red, and yellow. Find ways to insert some color, perhaps with a tie for men or scarf for women. Be creative, but subtle. Dressing all in black, navy, or brown with no accenting colors does not invite people to move toward you. Whenever I am closing a deal, I wear a specific color, and it's something you might enjoy doing yourself. Prior to your arrival at a company for your big-day interview, select a closing color and continue to wear it throughout the interview process until the deal is done. It will be your secret—but it might just help confirm your flawless fit.

After you carefully select what you are planning to wear on your big day, try on the whole outfit in advance and look at yourself in a full-length mirror, checking to be sure that every detail is exactly right. If something isn't, fix it before, not on, the big day. The flawless fit is your goal!

What Should I Take To and From the Interview?

Carry an attractive portfolio that contains original copies of your résumé. But give it to the person who is interviewing you only if that person hasn't been given an advance copy. Ideally, everyone who is interviewing you should have received your résumé before your arrival. There are two reasons not to distribute your résumé at the interview: First, you want the interviewer to read your Right Fit résumé before the interview in order to confirm that you are the Right Fit for the position. Second, you don't want to appear as if you are carrying your hat in your hand, seeking "work."

Your perceived image is very important. Depending on your profession, select and carry supporting documentation and examples of your craft. Arrange the portfolio so you can readily pull out what you need without fumbling. Everything you bring with you should reinforce that you are who you purport to be. Be prepared to leave your documentation with the human resources department, including transcripts, degrees, licenses, and certifications. Bring originals to show and request that they make copies, leaving originals only if absolutely required. Be thoughtful in selecting what examples of your craft to bring with you and the manner or purpose for which they are used. If you are a journalist, it makes obvious sense to bring examples of your published articles. Select those that would be of special interest to this particular employer because of subject matter and style. When you share the articles, it's important for you to explain exactly why you selected them. Do not assume that the interviewer will figure that out on your behalf.

Depending on your profession, it may not be readily apparent what examples of your craft are appropriate to share during the interview. My candidates have brought along business, marketing, and financial plans, as well as curriculum designs, architectural plans, and clinical protocols, among many other documents. Be very clear about your role in creating these exhibits, and give appropriate credit to others as well. Make sure you maintain confidentiality. Remove identifying information, such as company names, from the documents. By doing so you will broadcast your clear understanding that much corporate information is proprietary.

Candidates have often asked me whether they should jot down notes during the interview. I think it's important for you to carry a small notebook in your portfolio. Take it out at the beginning of each interview and have it ready in case the interviewer suggests something or someone you need to remember. Record those details, but otherwise spend your time during the interview listening and speaking rather than writing. Be sure to take a business card from every person who interviews you. Keep all material such as brochures, employee benefit information, and bios. You never know what you may need, especially when you are invited back.

As soon as you are alone after the interview, write down anything else you want to remember to follow up on when you return for subsequent interviews or have telephone or e-mail communications. Do not rely on your memory. It's very easy to forget details that could be important in closing the deal.

What Should I **Not** *Take to the Interview?*

Please do not bring your cell phone to the interview, even if you've turned it off. You want to clearly communicate the message that you have left all other business, whether professional or personal, outside the interview room. Maintain a single focus—the interview. Many people have their cell phones set to automatically answer. Can you imagine forgetting that the auto-answer is on? Picture this: During the interview, your current employer calls you. Your phone answers, and your employer listens to the entire interview. Do you believe that this could not happen? Well, it did. To avoid an unfortunate mishap, please do not bring your cell phone to the interview.

I think it's best not to bring general letters of reference to the interview. You want prospective employers to see references that are tailored to communicate the Right Fit for their particular position. If, sometime in the future, it's appropriate to share those general references in response to specifically relevant questions, share them then. Remember to stay focused on the fit—always. You never want to direct employers to areas of discussion that generate questions not related to the fit. Continue closing at all times.

What Should I Do After the Interview?

Following the interview, it's critically important to reinforce your Personal Brand. E-mailed thank-you notes are nothing new, and I don't recommend them. We all receive too much e-mail, and if sent electronically your thank-you note can easily be overlooked. Instead, send a lovely handwritten note on distinctive stationery, preferably matching your résumé stationery to maintain a consistent Personal Brand. For each interviewer, prepare a personally tailored note that triggers and reinforces the interviewer's memory of you. Mention a key point or two that was raised in your discussion. A general note is not effective and may be annoying because it will not reflect any imagination or real interest in the position on your part. I recommend that immediately following the interview you jot down the key points you want to incorporate in your personalized thank-you notes—mastering another step in closing by always planning ahead.

The Total Package:
The Entrepreneur Who Is the Flawless Fit

Entrepreneur William Ernest Brown and the Beverly Hills stationery store that bears his name are legendary. **For thirty-seven years, he has set a standard against which no one can compete, never bedeviled by the devil's details. Known in this country and abroad, attracting movie stars and moguls to his shop, courtly Mr. Brown, now seventy-seven, walks onto our stage to share his story with us.**

> My family has been in retail since the eighteenth century. I grew up in the jewelry business. Early in my career, I left my birthplace, Nova Scotia, in Canada, to go to New York City. I was not content living in a rather provincial place. In Manhattan, I worked for two prominent jewelers. I was Harry Winston's personal assistant, working with him directly. Then, at Mario Buccellati's, I worked directly with

his son. From both men, I learned an amazing amount about merchandising.

When I went to California on vacation, I decided to start my own business in Beverly Hills. But I didn't have enough money to go into the jewelry business. In the old days, jewelry and stationery were sold together. Both are created from engraved plates, which I learned about as a child. I knew enough about stationery to open a store as well as how to create designs. From the time I was a baby, my mother would draw in front of me and also hand me paper and pencil and encourage me to draw as well. At age five or six, I started taking art lessons and continued until I went to college, where I majored in business.

In 1970, when I opened my 400-square-foot stationery store in Beverly Hills, there were about twenty jewelry stores and one, not very good, stationery store. I had made the right decision. I was fortunate that my life partner, Jim Josoff, was by my side, supporting me while the store was getting underway. He later joined me in the business, becoming a great designer.

When I started my small store in the Courtyard on Canon Drive, I was alone. This is what I did. I listened very carefully to what the customers wanted. I did not try to sell them anything. I tried to give them exactly what they wanted. The sales grew very slowly. In the first month, I only took in thirty-five dollars. At that time, Volkswagen was very successful in the United States. They ran an ad that said that in 1947 they had sold two Volkswagens during the entire year. I cut out the ad, framed it, and put it above my desk. That was my inspiration to succeed. Gradually, by word of mouth, my sales increased. I was giving my customers what they wanted.

Charlotte Morrill, a brilliant designer, became my partner and we grew the business even more. With Charlotte's fresh ideas, we designed with an extra dimension. We advertised very little, but effectively. We ran one-inch, one-column, boxed-in teaser ads in the *Los Angeles Magazine* that looked like editorials—one in the front of the magazine, the second in the middle, and the third in the back. Each ad was different, and they asked questions such as:

> You mean you haven't visited Mr. Brown's
> little shop in the Courtyard?

The ads created a buzz. With the ads and word-of-mouth recommendations from satisfied customers, our client base grew beyond Beverly Hills to France, England, and Mexico. We were international! We outgrew our little store and expanded. Our clients included the most important names in the motion picture and television industries, and many business and society leaders. These clients knew that we respected their privacy and could trust us not to reveal their names to the press.

What is the secret to my success? A very good product, fair price, and very good service. Anticipate what the customer wants. Very often, the customer does not know what he or she wants. You have to elicit that information from the customer. Then give them something that fits their needs and significantly exceeds their expectations. The genius of my business is figuring out what the customers want. We do a lot of the work ourselves and stay until midnight if necessary in order to meet and exceed the customer's expectations. No matter what, the customer comes first.

The William Ernest Brown brand is expanding. In March 2006, I sold the business to the Vaniers, brilliant merchandisers who will create a national chain, keeping my name. I had no original intention of selling, but their concept appealed to me. What do I do now? At age seventy-seven, I go to the stationery store daily, continuing to interact with customers. And I've returned to my passion as a sculptor. I have exhibited my work internationally. I had a wonderful commission to do a seven-foot bronze monument to the first King of Norway, which the Queen of Norway unveiled in June 2007.

I look with admiration at my uncle, who died at his bench making jewelry at age ninety-seven, having made beautiful jewelry for over seventy-five years. I want to be as creative as he was for the rest of my life.

As a customer of Mr. Brown's for many years, I can confirm that he knows how to retain his clients. He exerts absolutely no pressure, produces a first-rate product, and always remembers who you are. No detail is ever too small to satisfy his customers, and no detail is overlooked. He is a man to remember.

Trigger Tip
William Ernest Brown

Let's forge ahead!

ACT III

Apply the Right Fit Method

CHAPTER ELEVEN

The Wrong Fit: Fix It or Flee

Your Goal: Probe before, after, and forever.

Probe Before

TRUST ME. Receiving an offer will make you feel *very* good about yourself. The message you receive is *we want you!* After you've taken some time to enjoy the initial excitement, ask yourself whether *you* really want *them*.

Don't forget that the fit needs to be right for both the employee and the employer. It's possible to recognize red flags early in the interview process, but you may not always be aware of their significance. Do not ignore those warning flags. Instead, evaluate their significance and decide what to do. You should not proceed to the offer stage if you have determined along the way that you will not accept it because you can't change elements of the offer that are unacceptable to you. Too often, however, candidates simply assume they can't change what is unacceptable. But if you Manage the Process effectively, you will be amazed at what you can do. Your goal is to evaluate the whole opportunity from a variety of perspectives to prevent accepting the wrong fit position. Why? Because it's easier to prevent a bad situation than to treat it.

Now we'll further hone your probing skills. Ultimately, you should be able to probe automatically, without thinking, in much the same way as you drive your car. To perfect your probing skills, I highly recommend studying the probing styles of journalists like Barbara Walters. Watching "tennis match" interviews will give you further insight into how professionals do it. Your goal is to become a "probing pro" in your own environment.

Let's look at potential red-flag areas in which you must probe, with an eye toward fixing problems before they start, prior to accepting the position. After talking with hundreds of wrong fit employees, I developed this list.

Commuting

You have to decide what is an acceptable commute via car, bus, train, or subway. For a few, the commute may even involve flying. You can negotiate a wide array of arrangements, depending on the extent to which you must be present in person. For one of my client-employers, I created a whole team of employees who worked from home. They had weekly meetings by telephone. The idea that the whole team would work from home evolved simply because the head of the team would not relocate, and he flew to the company's headquarters monthly to meet with his supervisor and other executives.

If you want to work one or two days a week from home, probe to find out whether this idea is feasible. Then, pitch your suggestion. Before you pitch, however, it's important to be very sure that the employer views you as the Right Fit. The employer will be far more open to doing things differently if indeed you are.

To find out about whether your physical presence is necessary on a daily basis, ask: **"When would we meet?"**

After you pitch this question, continue pitching until you obtain the information I describe below.

You want the supervisor to think divergently and share more information than the question elicits. Your goal is to elicit a response not only about the frequency of meetings, but also about the extent of supervision. You want the supervisor to share something of his or her management style. If you would be working with minimal supervision and little direct observation, then working at home one or two days a week might be possible. If you would be supervising a staff requiring minimal direct supervision, perhaps talking on the phone and e-mailing could work. It's up to you to figure out whether the supervisor's management style and philosophy are consonant with what you want to pitch. If they are not, then *do not* pitch your idea unless you know exactly how to overcome the objections you anticipate. In order to succeed, you'll need to read the supervisor with all your senses, analyzing both verbal and nonverbal cues. If you pitch properly, the response you seek is either "yes" or "let me find out whether we can work this out."

In the event that the answer is "no," you have three options: suggest working a four-day week with longer hours or flextime; move your household closer to your "new" employer; or decide not to proceed further with the opportunity. Do not accept a position if you already find yourself mumbling and grumbling about the commute. This is clearly the wrong fit, and you will not be happy.

Responsibilities, Expectations, and Hours

Find out early on in the interview process exactly what your responsibilities will be. You do not want surprises. Sometimes the employer, as we previously discussed, is not crystal clear about what the responsibilities will be. If that's the case, then the expectations as well as the hours needed to satisfy the responsibilities could also be unclear. I recommend that you probe for clarity, but, ultimately, you may need to delineate in writing the responsibilities (tasks) and expectations (achievements) for the position. Create a Blended Blueprint for the first year. List three to six major tasks (what you need to do), weight the importance of each task, and articulate benchmarks of achievement with targeted completion dates. Then, make two copies of the blueprint, one for you and the other for the employer. On *your* blueprint *only*, calculate the number of hours you will need to work each week to meet these benchmarks. Be realistic.

Next, share the blueprint without the estimated work hours with the employer, explaining that clarity is your goal. Suggest a date on which you will send the blueprint, and ask if you should e-mail it or send it via postal mail. Then, arrange a meeting to discuss the blueprint, either in person or by phone. Make no assumptions. Remember, no detail is too small. Use this document as a way to stimulate the employer's thinking with regard to mutually agreed-upon expectations and benchmarks. Reaching an agreement on the blueprint is critically important in preventing potential problems such as significant added responsibility without remuneration, unrealistic expectations, and unacceptably long hours. Again, it's your responsibility to take charge and Manage the Process. If you have the Right Fit supervisor, that person will be delighted that you have taken the initiative to create the blueprint.

If you cannot reach an agreement on the specifics of the blueprint following your meeting, do not accept the position on the presumption that you can figure this out later. If you are disenchanted during the engagement period, getting married is *not* the solution you seek. Consider this opportunity the wrong fit and press on.

Culture and Peers

Every organization has its own culture. You must be comfortable in the environment in which you will be working. A family-owned company is very different from a Fortune 500 company. It's important to find out before you accept the position whether the culture and peers are the Right Fit for you. If you are a new graduate just entering the work world, it may be difficult to figure this out because you have not had enough experience to create a set of standards that would incorporate the cultural components. More seasoned professionals may have experience in only one type of business culture, perhaps not in the one to which they are considering making a change. The best way to evaluate whether the culture and peers are right for you is to experience the situation during the interview process.

- **Observe the Employees.** Direct observation is as important as probing. Look at people's faces. Do they look happy, relaxed, involved? If they look forlorn, overstressed, or uninvolved, those are red flags that need to be investigated. Do the employees interact with each other in a warm, friendly manner? How do they greet you? I once placed a candidate in an environment that was openly hostile to her. She was replacing an internal candidate who had temporarily held the management position for which my candidate was being interviewed. That internal candidate behaved dreadfully toward my candidate. Quite skillfully, however, my candidate overwhelmed the internal candidate with kindness, wooing her over to some degree. Additionally, the client-employer's management team worked hard to console the internal candidate and to support my candidate, her replacement. My candidate visited the employer a number of times prior to accepting the offer to ensure that she was avoiding a wrong-fit situation. And I'm delighted to report that the placement worked successfully. After many years, she is still there. Remember to observe the company's employees as carefully as you can, identifying and addressing the red flags to determine what can and cannot be fixed.

- **Probe the Peers.** Prior to accepting a position, it's your responsibility to be sure you meet with those people with whom you will be interacting regularly. Normally, you will meet with some of your peers during the interview process because *they* will be interviewing you. Sometimes, however, this may not occur. If you do not meet the people you'll work with during the interview, request a meeting with them to ensure that they are individuals with whom you can work successfully.

  Prior to meeting with your peers, create a list of questions to help probe how things are accomplished in their company's or organization's culture. Again, you are trying to determine whether their style and approach is the Right Fit for you. If it is not, it's time to determine what is engraved in stone and what can be changed. To what extent are they flexible, and are they flexible on issues that are vitally important to you?

  Recall what you *observed* about the employees. Ask questions that help you investigate the particulars of your observations. For example, if your overall impression is that the employees are overstressed,

Say: **"I observed happy faces as I was walking around. This must be a wonderful work environment."**

If you receive no response, probe further.

Ask: **"Why do you enjoy working here?"**

Try to determine whether what you observe is a happy or unhappy kind of stress. If the stress is due to unreasonable pressure to perform, you need to know that. Your goal is to prevent yourself from accepting a situation you can't live with.

■ **Probe the Direct Reports.** If you are pursuing a management position, you must meet those people who will report directly to you. When you meet these "direct reports," use the meeting or meetings as an opportunity to confirm what you have been told about the position and to learn more about the company's culture. For example, if the last person who held the position you're on the brink of accepting left after a short time, find out why. Then, probe further back in time to determine whether this is a pattern. Direct reports, as a rule, love sharing information. Just sit back and listen, observe, and evaluate. You'll be able to determine rapidly whether you can work successfully with the direct reports in that organization's culture.

■ **Probe to Assess Growth Potential.** Evaluate whether there is a growth opportunity beyond the position for which you are being interviewed.

You don't want to feel "stuck" in your new
position because you can't move up. If this
happens, you will quickly begin to view your
position as the wrong fit. If growth potential is
of significant importance to you, probe your
new supervisor gently. For example, if the next
logical step up for you would be moving into
the supervisor's own position, explore the
company's overall growth plans with him or
her, posing what appears to be a general question.

Ask: **"Five years from now, what do you
think will be different about this company?"**

Notice how I formed a question to elicit a
broad spectrum of responses. The response to
the question may surprise you. The supervisor
might say, "I will no longer be here because I
am planning to retire. My position could be
yours. I am looking for a successor." It is not
uncommon for employers to search for succes-
sors. But they may not share this information
with you unless you probe. Some employers
want to see their potential replacements in
action, prior to sharing their own plans or their
thoughts about an employee's long-term
future. The bottom line is that you must gather
the information that you need to assess in
advance whether the position's growth potential is right for you. Having said that, keep in
mind that you always need to be ready for
unexpected changes like mergers or acquisitions.

Note that I am not suggesting that probing is
a cure-all that can prevent you from accepting
a wrong-fit position. Probing simply enables

you to learn a lot about an employer so you can determine whom you will be "marrying" if you accept the offer, and sometimes it allows you to fix the fit before the deal is done.

Probe to Fix

Some situations in a work environment can be fixed, others cannot. It's crucial to your professional career for you to learn how to recognize the difference. Otherwise, you may leave one position for another only to find out that the same challenges are repeating themselves.

Is your challenge the relationship with your supervisor?

Frequently, employees make the assumption that their supervisors know and understand the same things they do. Some do, but, in truth, some don't. To prevent any misunderstandings about your performance, be sure to write a monthly or quarterly report outlining what you have achieved. Discuss the process only minimally—the specific work you actually do—so your supervisor can visualize you doing what you do day-to-day. Instead, the focus of your report should be on outcome—the end result of your work.

After you've e-mailed the report or presented it personally, arrange a time to meet and discuss it. At that meeting, probe to be sure the supervisor has read the report, and probe to find out the extent to which the supervisor is satisfied with your performance. If he or she has performance issues, discuss and agree on solutions during this meeting. I'm always amazed when employees call me, explaining their performance difficulties and swearing that signs of the supervisor's dissatisfaction were not readily apparent. Submitting and discussing your reports with your supervisor will reduce the probability of unpleasant surprises.

Are you leaving your supervisor out of the loop?

Once, when I was conducting my Wrong Fit Workshop, I knew intuitively that a woman telling a story about her difficulty with a supervisor was omitting some vital information about their relationship. After some probing of my own, she explained that she regularly played golf with her supervisor's supervisor—but *not* with her supervisor. Why not make the golf game a threesome? By omitting her supervisor, she had created a problem, which she sheepishly agreed she needed to fix. Prevent problems; don't create them.

Is your supervisor leaving you out of the loop?

If your supervisor is not inviting you to meetings to which you should be invited, be proactive. Arrange a time to speak with your supervisor about another matter. In the course of your conversation, slip in a statement like this: **"I'm sure it was an oversight that I wasn't invited to Tuesday's meeting."** Say nothing more and wait for a response. You goal is to learn why you were not invited and to prevent it from happening again. Do not allow "oversights" to continue without fixing the situation. Make it clear to your supervisor that in order for you to perform at a high level, you need to be an integral part of the team and that "oversights" are not acceptable to you. If you *don't* speak up, the supervisor might make the assumption that it's acceptable to you to be left out of the loop. If you do not speak up, you may ultimately encounter a situation you cannot fix, requiring you to flee.

Think about whether you are doing something to invite exclusion. For example, are you talking too much at meetings, or not enough? You want to contribute to but not to dominate those gatherings. Think about your behaviors that may invite exclusion.

Is your challenge the relationship with your peers?

Every person with whom you work cannot love you and

may not even like you. Your goal is to develop amicable relationships with your peers so that they treat you with respect. When you start a new position, carefully lay the groundwork for developing peer relationships. First, listen to others, then gradually share some personal information. Don't use your peers as sounding boards for either personal or professional problems. In fact, don't vent your complaints to anyone! The idea that you can successfully confide in anyone at work is a myth—you cannot. *Trust No One!*

Initially, do not rush to share your new ideas. Peers can easily become threatened. First, establish amicable peer relationships, then introduce your ideas gradually. Your peers will now be ready to listen to you because you are a colleague who does not pose a threat.

If your peers are currently adversarial or confrontational, that is not a simple matter to fix. If you've done what I recommended *not* to do, stop now. Be patient and watch to see if the atmosphere changes. The extent of your peers' alienation will determine whether the situation can be fixed.

Is your challenge the relationship with your direct reports?

Initially, it is important to assure those employees who report to you that you want to get acquainted with them and to learn what they do. Make it clear that you do not intend to make any immediate changes. Meet with each direct report and other key team members privately in order to learn what makes each person tick. Concurrently, probe to learn more about how that employee feels about his or her position, the organization, and the supervisor who preceded you.

From the very beginning, set the stage to show you care about your employees. If you do, you'll be there for each other down the line when the need arises. When I was working at the National Institutes of Health, some of my employees were downsized due to budget constraints. Those employees continued to come to work, without being paid, because they knew I needed them. I told them I would write a letter to the secretary of Health and Human Services in hopes of having them reinstated. With the help of a superb executive assistant, we pitched our plight, pleaded our cause, and won. My employees were reinstated, and I treasured their loyalty to me.

If you are currently having difficulty with some of your direct reports, it is your responsibility to determine the cause. In a one-on-one meeting, discuss the issues and resolve them immediately as best you can. Otherwise, they may "undo" you.

When to Flee

I have focused on preventing challenges because it is better to prevent problems than to attempt to fix them. But it is vitally important for you to recognize those times when staying in a position is, or soon could be, detrimental to your health. Some of the employees who attend my Wrong Fit Workshop are already physically ill. Don't allow that to happen to you. Begin searching for a new position before you reach that stage. But note that I don't recommend leaving your current position before you have a new one. Remember Laurie? I convinced her to stay a while longer in the position in which she was miserable, during which time I coached her to stardom, something that would have been nearly impossible in her case if she had been unemployed. For some, fleeing is the only solution to their pain. **Remember Ned? Let's find out how he dealt with career pain that otherwise might have overwhelmed him.**

During my final years at the bank, other people wrote speeches for me. Other people, in fact, were doing everything for me, including getting and doing the business. All I did was supervise and attend meetings. And therein lay the rub.

I was fifty years old. But I could just as well have been seventy, given what I was now doing—or not doing. My peers at the bank, all good MBAs, had made "not doing" their career objective. They strove to reach a position where they were no longer caught in the performance trap. Others had to perform for them, and they paid the price for nonperformance. Oh sure, you might in the end pay a price for the ongoing nonperformance of those for whom you were responsible, but that was nothing like being on the front line each day and being judged on the result.

I actually loved that daily challenge. And my final three years of "not doing" at the bank became increasingly frustrating. There was no way I could tolerate this situation for ten or fifteen more years. At the beginning of my twenty-second year, I told the chairman of the bank that I intended to leave and start my own business. I told him why, and he simply could not understand. What's more, he was convinced that good sense and a substantial raise would prevail. They didn't.

I left the bank on Bastille Day, 1986. With my own money and some considerable financial support from friends and former clients, I formed a merchant banking and financial advisory firm specializing in corporate finance and providing seed capital for developers of new power and chemical-processing projects. The staff consisted of one analyst and an administrative assistant. What had I got myself into? And what was I to do now? Understand—as I certainly didn't at the outset—that I hadn't done any real work for many years. There were always the Bills, Johns, and Janes who, among other things, answered the phones, sorted the mail, paid the bills, dealt with suppliers, read and analyzed proposals, made new business presentations, reviewed first drafts of documents, and negotiated the basic terms of every transaction in which the firm was involved. What I *did* understand, although not fully, was the importance of the bank's uniform in getting and doing business—as opposed to just presenting myself and the record of my achievements.

I understood such importance intellectually, but the fact of it—especially when presenting to new clients—was both frustrating and disheartening.

Suck it up, son, I said to myself. You made the choice. The family, your employees are depending on you, to say nothing of the investors in your firm. The answer to my question of what to do now was to recognize what needed to be done—and to build a record not on who I was formerly, but rather on who and what I was now.

I was the CEO and principal owner of a new merchant banking and financial advisory firm. The only deals I was likely to get were ones that the larger and more established firms did not want. My immediate task would be to cull from the discards and rejects the one deal that would serve as a springboard for better and stronger deals. It took almost two months for me to find such a deal, and nearly three years for us to bring that deal to a successful conclusion. We stumbled many times along the way, but the commitment of my associates never wavered. The prize, after all, was more than just a fee or compensation for missed paydays; the prize was survival and the promise of a future.

It is twenty years later. We are still in a thriving business. That first deal did, in fact, bring better and stronger deals, but—as a wise woman once told me—investment banking is the hardest way to make easy money. Some of our deals failed, to be sure, testing both our confidence and durability, but we have overcome our failures and built an enviable record of success. The creed we live by, however, is that you are only as good as your last deal. The last deal is still pending. The story goes on. Success breeds success. Your reputation precedes you.

When Ned concluded in chapter seven that he had "arrived," did you think the bank would be his final resting place?

If you said "no," you are a shrewd observer. If you said "yes," please reread the first part of Ned's story. Notice his pace and energy level. Ned is a doer and an entrepreneur at heart; staying at the bank throughout his career would indeed have been a wrong fit for him.

What happened at the bank? He ascended to a level where he did nothing. Becoming the chairman of the bank, the logical next step, was not a solution for him either. He would ascend to more responsibility, but that would bring even more "not doing."

Ned had two choices: endure his pain or leave. For Ned, the right solution was to become a "real" entrepreneur, building a business, which by now has been thriving for more than twenty years. Along the way, his energy and determination never faltered.

Should Ned have left the bank early in his career? If he had, he would not have built the strong relationships and skills necessary to grow his new business.

Think about what the right solution is for you in your current position. Probe yourself to determine what you want and need. Do not sit on the fence. If it is the wrong fit, fix it. If you cannot fix it, get ready to flee.

Trigger Tip
Do not sit on the fence

Let's carry on to victory!

CHAPTER TWELVE

The Ax Is Falling? Proceed to Search

Your Goal:
Analyze the ax, conclude, and advance.

AT ANY POINT in your career, you can re-evaluate your Core Identity and decide to make a change. Remember how Ned made a dramatic shift from employee to entrepreneur after more than twenty years as an employee? Similarly, you have the right *and* the power to say, "This position is no longer the Right Fit for me." In Ned's case, he left the bank because he wanted to become a *doer* again. It is better for you to Manage the Process, determining your own destiny, than to await a falling ax, which could leave you ill, disrupt your family, and cause other serious problems.

Let me ask a simple question: *Who holds the employment ax?* If your answer is the employer, you've made an erroneous assumption. In fact, the wielders of the ax are you, the employer, or both. But in this chapter, let's focus on you—the employee.

Who axed Ned? *He* did. The bank—his employer—wanted him to stay, offering him a higher salary if he would remain in his position. But he was resolute. He took the risk and left, after lining up investors for his new company. Ned planned ahead, paving the way to success.

If you have professional challenges in your current situation that you cannot resolve using the Right Fit Method, then it's time to Proceed to Search. If, for example, your employer decides that you do not "fit in" for whatever reason, and life at work is becoming increasingly difficult, even intolerable, then it's time to Proceed to Search. Do not wait for the employer to terminate you, even if you believe the employer's perception of you is not accurate—this is not a question of right and wrong. Don't try to deny the reality of the situation. Accept it and proceed. You can waste lots of time and energy complaining about your employer. Instead, find the Right Fit situation now.

Be aware of the telltale signs of financial problems within your current organization, including impending downsizing. If you hear rumors that your company is having financial problems, or your paychecks are late or have bounced, do not bury your head in the sand. *Proceed to Search.* If you hear what appears to be factual information about an impending merger or acquisition, Proceed to Search. Who knows who the new decision makers will be and how you will be affected?

The bottom line is that you must take charge and manage your own professional future. If the signposts indicate that your position is on shaky ground, you must act. Using the Right Fit Method, Proceed to Search. But note something very important. I'm not recommending that you take a new position. If the reason that motivated the search does not materialize, you may not need to leave your current position. For example, let's say the merger never materialized, or it did and you've been offered another position in the company that you truly do want. If, in the meantime, you also have found a new Right Fit position, then the choice to stay or go is yours, not your current employer's.

Proceed to Search for What?

When you are at a career crossroads, benefit from the situation and re-evaluate your Core Identity using your *Annual Core Identity Check-up*, which is waiting for you in chapter four. Remember not to begin scattering your résumé around the world. Stay focused, determining your next step precisely. If you no longer want to be an employee and have been toying with the idea of becoming an entrepreneur, perhaps this is the right time for you to plan and proceed.

When we left Jason in chapter six, he had downsized himself again and was at a crossroads in his career. This time, he decided that working for someone else was not the Right Fit for him.

> I had a lot of free time now that I didn't have a job, so I did a lot of reading. One of my friends from Firstlook.com gave me the book *Atlas Shrugged*, and I started reading it. I did not know of Ayn Rand, or her philosophy, but it validated everything I had done throughout my whole life. She talked about meritocracy and the value of living by a code of reason. She spoke of the virtue of selfishness and living up to the highest standards available.
>
> I was inspired again. I knew what I had to do. I loved the small company feel, and I loved to teach. I was going to bring those two loves together and start my own company. But should I teach the CPA exam? I knew it well. I had been doing it for a few years now, but I didn't love it. What I did love though, was the SAT, which I loved because of its full name. It's the SAT Reasoning Test. To succeed on the exam, you need to use reasoning, logic, and analytical thinking. I valued reasoning above all else, so it appeared that I was destined to do this.

Starting my own company in a new industry was a huge risk, but I felt prepared. I learned what didn't work at my other companies, so I was ready for the challenge. To have a successful company, I needed four things: an understanding of the market; a competitive advantage; a solid financial model, and a talented management team. I spent a few months doing market research on the SAT prep industry and put together a financial model. My CPA background came in handy here. I hired a few of the top-notch employees I had worked with at my previous jobs, and, together, we set up our competitive advantages. We decided that one-on-one tutoring would be our niche, and the company got its start. My old marketing guru (who had given me *Atlas Shrugged*) was my right hand in building the company. She came up with the name, Eureka One-on-One Review, and the logo. I wrote the materials, and we tested them on my youngest brother and his friends. They were our beta students, and we learned a great deal about how to present reasoning skills to high-school students. After about a year of planning, research, and preparation, we launched to the public.

The mantra of Eureka, written on the bottom of every piece of stationery we had, was *Expect Success*. It was the standard that I lived by, and the standard I expected from my employees. I was *not* an easy boss to work for. Because my standards were so high, an employee could never exceed my expectations, only meet them. My first ten employees and tutors were all prior contacts of mine who knew my code and knew what it took to work for me. They helped me build a great reputation for my company, and I was soon searching to hire more people. This was tough for me to do. There was a certain style I was looking for and it wasn't easy to find. I would interview all day and come up empty-handed. My marketing guru told me that I couldn't hold others to the same standards I held myself to. But I disagreed.

My company was in a flourishing market, had successful tutoring materials, impressive financial margins, but yet I needed more people to manage the demand I was building. I learned in the past to *Never Settle*, so I spent the next few months interviewing, interviewing, interviewing. Eventually, I found the right people, with the right work ethic, who valued the things I did. I gave each employee the same speech the day he or she started. "I value reason above all else. If you work with this as your backbone and know that independent thought, based in reason, is of the utmost importance, you will succeed with my company. If not, we won't be together for long." I have been told that this is an intimidating speech, but it is only intimidating to those who don't live by a code of reason.

Eureka grew by leaps and bounds in its first years. I spent ninety hours per week working on it, and, somehow, my wife stood by me again. She understood my passion and respected my vision. She was patient and acted as my rock during the difficult times. The general public doesn't realize the trials and tribulations of running your own business. It is the best and worst thing you'll ever do. I shrugged off all our success, and I took every failure personally. My standards forced me to live like this. It wasn't healthy, but it made me push my company to the next level.

In year two, Eureka hit the year-end revenue goal on July 7th. I was excited at this accomplishment, but only for ten minutes. I knew not to rest on my laurels. *Avoid contentment.* I continued to work the hours needed to exceed expectations and prove that this was a successful business model and a profitable company.

In year three, I shifted my priorities to expansion. People sometimes equate expansion with success. There is a correlation, but it is closer to 0 than 1. My dot.com company had expanded across the United States and overseas to Europe. I learned about starting up in different regions, even though we didn't have a profitable model. We spent $50 million and ran out of capital quickly. At Eureka, I wanted my expansion to be slow and smart. We expanded to San Francisco and San Diego. These are affluent markets, similar to Los Angeles, which value education highly. Many people asked me why I wouldn't expand further. Well, I knew that California was the world's fifth largest economy. And until Eureka was the number-one provider of test prep in California, there was no need to dilute resources.

Today, Eureka has over 200 tutors across California. In my previous dot.com ventures, it cost me $1.10 to earn $1.00 in revenue, while at Eureka, it only costs me 23 cents to earn that same dollar. Running on margins of 77 percent, Eureka has been called a spectacular success by some, but not by me. One day I might use that term, but not one day soon.

Jason clearly articulated his vision to become an entrepreneur with a specific mission. Like Ned, he planned meticulously. He created a solid financial model and hired a talented management team. Driven by his high standards, Jason created a company that remains to this day a spectacular success. Becoming a notable entrepreneur is not an easy task. Be sure you have the "stuff" to do it before proceeding.

Proceed to Search

If you have made the decision to seek another position and you have precisely identified the Right Fit position you want, you are ready to Proceed to Search. To achieve your goal in an efficient manner, it's time to plan a campaign. To do that, it's essential for you to understand the options that are open to you.

Before reviewing and evaluating these options, let me stress the importance of never using your current position as a place from which to search for a new position. (The only exception is if your current employer has explicitly stated that you can do so, but that circumstance is, of course, not the norm.)

In an earlier chapter, I mentioned that employers can view your e-mail messages. Does the same hold true for voice-mail? Let me share with you my firsthand experience with voice-mail. I once left a message for a candidate on his office voice-mail system, stating the details of the time of his upcoming interview, and purposely omitting my client-employer's name. The next day that candidate's employer, the CEO, left me a message asking me to call him. When I did, I learned that some-one—obviously a person who disliked my candidate—had for-warded my voice-mail message to the CEO. The employer told me he would fire the person who forwarded the voice-mail to him if he could identify him or her. And during the course of our conversation, the CEO became my next candidate. An-other company was acquiring his company, and he was ready to Proceed to Search.

Tampering with voice-mail in this situation backfired on the person who did the tampering, and it reinforced a valuable lesson: no piece of equipment at work—phone, computer, or fax—should be used for your private business.

Search Firms: An Insider's View

You would be amazed by the number of résumés search firms receive. Surely, enough résumés are sent to search firms to wallpaper the inside of all Donald Trump's real estate hold-ings and more.

I have learned that most employees and many employers do not understand how search firms function. Employers, not candidates, hire search firms. If the employer signs an agree-ment with a "retained" search firm, that employer has agreed to pay a fee, with an initial payment up front to begin the search. Sometimes, the whole fee is paid even if the employer does not hire a candidate presented by the search firm. If the employer signs an agreement with a "contingency" search firm, the employer only pays a fee to the search firm if he hires a candidate presented by that search firm.

What is the impact on the candidate of the contractual arrangement between the search firm and the employer?
If the search will be conducted on a "retained" basis, usually only one firm does the search and has what is known as an exclusive. If it will be done on a "contingency" basis, the employer frequently hires more than one search firm to conduct the search. In some situations, the search could be both contingency and exclusive.

If a search consultant contacts you, ask these questions prior to agreeing to become a candidate for a specific search:

- Is your firm retained or contingency?
- Does your firm hold an exclusive on this search?

If the search firm holds an exclusive, this will enable the firm to Manage the Process and increase the probability of completing the search. There are no guarantees. The employer could, for example, decide to cancel the search due to a sudden internal decision to reorganize or enforce immediate budget cuts. Probe the search consultant further to determine whether the consultant's approach to the search is the Right Fit for you.

Ask: "Do you send a batch of résumés to the employer from which they select who they want to interview?"
Let's hope the answer you hear is "no." Why? It's important for the search consultant to set the stage for the employer

to meet the Right Fit candidate. Otherwise, the employer is likely to compare the candidates, rather than evaluate each one against a set of standards. If you and the search consultant believe you are the Right Fit candidate for a specific position, and he or she uses the "batch approach," ask to be presented either first or last, if the employer is interviewing a group of candidates on the same day. Ideally, last is best. If you are not part of a group presentation, ask the search consultant to present only one candidate at a time, requesting again to be either first or last. In this case, first is best if you are the flawless fit. You want the employer to *see* you as the flawless fit and stop shopping. The employer may well tell the search consultant not to present any more candidates.

Ask: "Can you explain how we will work together?"

It's important to know whether the search consultant will guide you in crafting a Right Fit résumé for the position as well as prep you for your interviews and provide employer feedback after the interviews.

Ask: "How will you represent me?"

Find out whether the search consultant will pitch you—rather than simply send your résumé—and discuss the pitch with you prior to presenting you. Determine whether the search consultant will represent your interests to the employer, negotiating the offer for you.

In general, is it a good idea to mass mail—via e-mail, post, or fax—your résumé to search firms?

Search firms will add your résumé to their databases. Usually, they will call you if you are or could be the Right Fit for a specific search. They also may call you requesting candidate referrals in your field. You must be very sure that the search firms to whom you send your résumé never send your résumé to any employers without your permission.

Right Fit Search Consultant

The questions I've posed will enable you to "test the waters," assessing whether the search consultant with whom you're speaking could be the Right Fit for you. The following is a list of behaviors that characterize a Right Fit search consultant.

- ■ Interviews you in depth to determine whether you are the Right Fit candidate for a specific position, and only proceeds if you are. No square pegs in round holes!

- ■ Identifies the employer, sharing all relevant information about the company and the position. Information is never vague, and the consultant knows many details.

- ■ Guides you in the preparation of your résumé to articulate in detail how you match the position. Reviews and comments on your résumé revisions until the Right Fit résumé is completed.

- ■ Coaches you prior to each day of interviewing, clearly explaining exactly what to do and how to act. Remember David, "The Imprisoned Candidate?" If I had not alerted him to refuse to discuss salary, he would have behaved incorrectly, making it very difficult for me to negotiate an offer for him.

- ■ Debriefs you after each day of interviewing and shares with you the employer's feedback to help strategize what to do next. If, for example, your chemistry and the employer's are not blending, discuss the situation with the search consultant to determine whether you can fix it. If so, strategize how to do it. If not, do not proceed.

■ Conducts in-depth reference checking, sharing with the employer complete written references, not summaries. It is very important for the employer to read firsthand the words of the references. Something is always lost when references are only summarized.

■ Negotiates the package for you. Takes the information that you provided—including all the devil's details, ranging from salary to relocation and any special needs—and negotiates on your behalf. Be sure to present your realistic requirements to the search consultant early on in your relationship. Remember, no surprises at the end, such as, "I forgot that I need to move my multimillion dollar art collection," or "I forgot to talk to my spouse and children about moving." It is amazing what candidates forget. Once, I had to explain to my client-employer that the candidate who had just accepted his offer couldn't find his wife and children. The candidate, with whom I had worked for many months, had indicated he had marital problems but had *not* disclosed that his family might not be moving with him. Only when I verified with the candidate the mailing address to which my client-employer would send the offer letter for this high-level position did I learn that he had left his wife and was now living with a girlfriend, who subsequently moved with him instead of his wife. Please remember to mention vital information that the search consultant needs to know.

■   Advises you about how to resign from your current position. Never resign until you have signed a written offer letter or have responded in writing to that offer, indicating that you accept the position. Accepting a verbal offer is not enough. I once had a client-employer who authorized me to extend an offer to my candidate. After I had done so and the candidate had accepted the offer, the employer called me again to say he had miscalculated the salary and was rescinding the offer. Fortunately, the candidate had not resigned yet, because I had warned him not to do so until he had a signed contract. Until you are holding a written offer letter that you have formally accepted, the deal is not done.

A word of caution. When you resign from your current position, I recommend that you submit a written letter of resignation to avoid any misunderstandings, but don't include the name of your new employer in that letter—or even mention it to a colleague at your current company. Be discreet. You want to be certain that your new employer hears nothing negative from someone at your former company. My motto is, prevent problems; don't treat them.

■   Stays by your side until you start your new position, attending to any final details to help you to transition into your new position.

Follows up during your first month to be sure
that all is well and guides you, as needed.

The Right Fit search consultant is a valuable intermediary between you and the employer. Use that conduit wisely. Keep in mind that the percentage of search firm placements is small in relation to the magnitude of candidate requests. Right Fit candidates are not necessarily found among the thousands of résumés housed in databases. Be prepared to receive a phone call or other type of communication from a search consultant that might lead to a Right Fit position.

To differentiate yourself from the pack of candidates who contact search firms and to show your Personal Brand, I recommend the following:

Research search firms to identify those that place candidates in your profession and industry. Call them and identify the Right Fit search consultant—the person (or persons) who places candidates like you. Be sure to prepare in advance two succinct pitches to present who you are when you call the search firm. Direct the first pitch to the receptionist to identify the right search consultant for you. When you speak with the search consultant, you will present your second pitch, in which you will summarize in one sentence who you are, carefully inserting one of your major accomplishments and stating the type of position you are seeking. Then, in the second sentence, ask: *Do you introduce candidates to your client-employers who are not targeted to fill a specific search?* Search consultants with established clients will be on the lookout for top talent who are the Right Fit to introduce to their clients. If the search consultant says, "yes," then work with that person to determine whether this can be done for you. Then ask: *Do you market candidates?* You are trying to find out if the firm will call employers on your behalf to present you, without having a specific search. From the search firm's perspective, you need to be strong enough to market—leading to placing you and/or picking up new searches.

I have given you new avenues to pursue in establishing relationships with search firms. Be creative and ethical. If you are working with more than one search firm, be sure to tell the other or others. If someone has extended him or herself on your behalf, treat that person with respect.

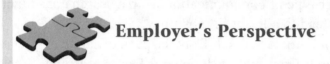 **Employer's Perspective**

The Right Fit search consultant (RFSC) for a specific employer can turn dreams into reality. Remember how Patti Rager described the growth of Nursing Spectrum, adding, *"Remember, it's all about the people. You must focus on your employees daily. Nothing happens unless they are devoted to your mission."* Without the Right Fit employees, Patti could not have built Nursing Spectrum into the company it is today, one whose publication reaches more than one million nurses.

The RFSC can save the employer time and money. The employer no longer needs to sort through mountains of résumés or interview numerous wrong fit candidates. Mindful of the employer's valuable time, the RFSC *only* presents Right Fit candidates. Sometimes, employers spend years searching on their own to fill a position. Even worse, they hire wrong fit candidates because they need people quickly to get the company's work done. Then, they fire those who are disasters. On the other hand, remember what Jason said about his high standards for hiring. He will *never* settle. Jason does not knowingly hire the wrong person, even if he is desperate.

When the employer and the RFSC build a relationship generated by successful placements, the employer shares more and more about the company. In turn, the RFSC becomes very knowledgeable about the organization's culture and management team. With this in-depth knowledge, the RFSC has what is needed to define, identify, and place flawless fit candidates. The RFSC functions as if he or she has an office inside the company.

The employer learns to rely on the RFSC to build the organization, by meeting scheduled deadlines to present and place Right Fit candidates. My candidates tell me that they gravitate to the other candidates I have placed in the same organization. Why? They all match the blueprint that I created. Their professions may or may not be the same; it's not the profession that's bringing them together. Their interpersonal skills, values, and cultural fit are flawlessly matched and that's what draws them to each other. When they have internal challenges, they turn to each other for support, and, when necessary, they call me. Employees with a strong internal support system enjoy going to work and stay longer in their positions.

When the RFSC presents you to the employer, what do the employers expect? A flawless fit, of course. Meet that expectation.

How to Broadcast Your Availability

Imagine that you are running for office. To win, you must design an effective, targeted campaign. Designing and implementing that campaign is a wonderful opportunity for you to practice and perfect competing with yourself. Jason is a superb example of someone who focuses relentlessly on his standards, consistently raising them. What's he doing? Competing with himself. Ned, Doyle, and Patti compete with themselves as well. I want *you* to compete with *yourself*.

Looking for a new position can be drudgery. If you adopt the attitude that you will make the process pleasurable and proceed accordingly, the results will astound you. An upbeat attitude draws people toward you.

Be very sure that you are comfortable with your Core Identity before you begin designing your campaign. Otherwise, you won't know what to broadcast, or you may say something vague, which won't be effective.

Design and Execute Your Campaign

- **Formulate the pitch.** Let's start with the basic pitch, which you will tailor to match the situation. Initially, you must decide what you want to tell the people whom you will contact about your interest in finding a new position. Keep the message simple and brief: **"I think it's time for me to pursue a new growth opportunity. I am ready to take on more responsibility as the [state the title of the position or positions]."**

  For example, you could express your interest in becoming the director of marketing or vice president of marketing. If you're currently a director, you may want to pursue a lateral move in a larger organization than your current company, or a vice president position in a smaller company. Your goal is to cast a broad net with specific targets. If you cast a narrow net, you may screen out opportunities you should pursue. You want to be flexible and open to possibilities, but also be clear on your criteria for the Right Fit position.

- **Make a list of key contacts.** Call your references first, telling them that you are calling to update them on your status. Then, broadcast your pitch, adjusting it to fit each person with whom you speak. Then, think back and reflect on the supervisors and colleagues with whom you have worked. Select those who know your work well, who admire and respect you, and who enjoy connecting people with each other. Ideally, you should have stayed in touch with a significant number of those contacts through e-mail, phone calls, and holiday cards. If not, when you call, catch up first before broadcasting your pitch. If you launch into your pitch immediately, it will appear that you are only calling to "use" the person, a message you do not want to communicate. There is no substitute for the expression of genuine caring for people. If you care about others, they will care about you in return. Recently, someone quite happily told me that she liked to fire people. How do you imagine her lack of empathy will catch up with her?

  Be sure to arrange a time to follow up with people who indicate that they will pursue possible leads. For example, perhaps one of your contacts has heard of someone resigning from a position for which you would be just right. Calling employers after someone resigns, but prior to the advertising of the position or the hiring of a search firm to conduct the search, is a very opportune time. Don't allow Right Fit unadvertised positions to slip by without action. Time is of the essence in this situation.

Call or drop an e-mail message every two weeks to those contacts who do not have leads— at least not yet. Be visible but not annoying; sometimes there's a fine line between the two. You need to be the judge, based on your specific relationships with your contacts.

Selectively identify family members and friends to whom you want to pitch your broadcast. Be sure to make a list before calling. And be sure to track all your telephone calls. Tracking is extremely important. The goal is to be sure that the pitching is sufficient to achieve your objectives. Sometimes you may think that you are doing more than you actually are, and it's vital for you to know that. The only way to find out is to track your performance, and telephone calls are the foundation of your campaign to effectively implement the Right Fit Method.

Determine your goals first. Then, increase them weekly, learning to compete with yourself by raising the bar, just as you do at the gym when you lift lighter weights first before gradually increasing to heavier weights.

To execute your campaign, determine what is right for you to do initially and then accelerate. Start thinking about the number of phone calls you are comfortable making daily. Phone calls, especially cold calls, are not a delightful activity for many people. Those who enjoy cold calling knowingly select professions that require it.

- **Respond to advertised positions.** In chapters six and seven, I described how to respond to

an advertised position. It may be tempting to
revert to old behaviors such as taking the
shotgun approach, wildly e-mailing into
cyberspace. But you are better than that, and I
encourage you to value who you are. Identify
those advertised positions that appear to be the
Right Fit. Call the employer or search firm to
investigate further, gathering as much information as you can about the Right Fit for each
position.

■ **Post yourself on the Internet.** There's no
question that posting your résumé on the
Internet provides enormous visibility. But if
you decide to post, I recommend that you omit
personal information, including your name,
home address, telephone number, and current
employer. Even if you are unemployed, I
recommend the same approach. If you overex-
pose yourself, this will hinder, not help you.
You do not want employers to say, "I keep
seeing this same résumé. Pass. This person is
not for me!" You also want to avoid appearing
desperate. If you are working and post your
résumé with identifying information, you risk
your current employer finding you on the
Internet and discovering that you are searching
for a new position.

■ **Send your unsolicited résumé to search
firms.** I recommend selectively sending your
résumé to search firms that focus on your
industry. For example, if you work in manufac-
turing, select search firms that have manufac-
turing clients. Research the search firms to

determine the Right Fit for you to increase the possibility that you'll receive a phone call from them. How does sending your résumé fit in with the cold calling I just discussed to differentiate yourself from others? Design a strategy to incorporate both approaches.

■   **Attend professional meetings.** Participating in professional meetings can be beneficial, especially if you present a paper. Your goal is visibility. Prior to each professional meeting, identify key people with whom you want to speak and arrange in-person meetings with them. Perhaps a specific company interests you or an advertised position has caught your eye. Do as much advance planning as you can prior to the meeting to make the event a worthwhile investment of your time.

   After each professional meeting, be sure to follow up with the key people you had discussions with, as well as those you met in passing. In my experience, the post-meeting follow-up is frequently not done in a systematic manner. Remember, you are always closing. If you want people to remember you, stay in touch to reinforce who you are. You never know when the Right Fit position may suddenly pop up, and your recent e-mail or phone call will trigger someone's memory of you for this position.

Self-Compete Hot and Cold Call Score Card

For one month, I want you to record the total number of phone calls you make each day to search for a new position. Then, break them down into two categories: hot calls and cold calls. Hot calls are people you know and cold calls are people you do not know. Your goals are to:

- Increase the total number of calls.
- Increase the number of hot calls.
- Increase the number of cold calls.

After you have spoken with the contact once and you call back a second time, consider this a hot call. Concurrently, you will increase your number of hot calls and cold calls. Don't stop making cold calls simply because there are a lot of hot calls to which you are attending. Make no assumptions! The promise of a position is not a closed deal. Never stop cold calling until the deal is closed.

Be sure to meet the goals I have set for you. If you have any problems, don't give up. If you need another week or two to meet the goals, take that time, but you shouldn't need more than two extra weeks. Try to meet the original goals. Use the extra weeks as a back-up plan. And trust me. You will feel great as you achieve your calling goals.

Now, review your **Self-Compete Hot and Cold Call Score Cards,** noting the goals. Then, design your campaign. Proceed and good luck!

Trigger Tip
Compete with yourself

Let's challenge the ax!

SELF-COMPETE HOT AND COLD CALL SCORE CARD*	
Week 1 Goals: Total 30 Hot 15 Cold 15	
Record the total number of phone calls each day. Then, the number of hot and cold calls.	Record the person's name, company, and phone number.

Monday   Total _____
                       Hot   _____
                       Cold _____	

Tuesday   Total _____
                       Hot   _____
                       Cold _____	

Wednesday   Total _____
                       Hot   _____
                       Cold _____	

Thursday   Total _____
                       Hot   _____
                       Cold _____	

Friday   Total _____
                       Hot   _____
                       Cold _____	

Saturday   Total _____
                       Hot   _____
                       Cold _____	

Sunday   Total _____
                       Hot   _____
                       Cold _____	

*Reproduce table to enlarge to provide more space to write.	

SELF-COMPETE HOT AND COLD CALL SCORE CARD*	
Week 2 Goals:	Total 45 Hot 20 Cold 25
Record the total number of phone calls each day. Then, the number of hot and cold calls.	Record the person's name, company, and phone number.

Monday   Total _____
                      Hot   _____
                      Cold _____	

Tuesday   Total _____
                      Hot   _____
                      Cold _____	

Wednesday Total _____
                      Hot   _____
                      Cold _____	

Thursday   Total _____
                      Hot   _____
                      Cold _____	

Friday   Total _____
                      Hot   _____
                      Cold _____	

Saturday   Total _____
                      Hot   _____
                      Cold _____	

Sunday   Total _____
                      Hot   _____
                      Cold _____	

*Reproduce table to enlarge to provide more space to write.	

SELF-COMPETE HOT AND COLD CALL SCORE CARD*	
Week 3 Goals:	Total 65 Hot 25 Cold 40
Record the total number of phone calls each day. Then, the number of hot and cold calls.	Record the person's name, company, and phone number.
Monday Total _____ Hot _____ Cold _____	
Tuesday Total _____ Hot _____ Cold _____	
Wednesday Total _____ Hot _____ Cold _____	
Thursday Total _____ Hot _____ Cold _____	
Friday Total _____ Hot _____ Cold _____	
Saturday Total _____ Hot _____ Cold _____	
Sunday Total _____ Hot _____ Cold _____	
*Reproduce table to enlarge to provide more space to write.	

SELF-COMPETE
HOT AND COLD CALL SCORE CARD*

Week 4 Goals:	Total 80 Hot 30
	Cold 50

Record the total number of phone calls each day. Then, the number of hot and cold calls.	Record the person's name, company, and phone number.

Monday   Total _____
             Hot _____
             Cold _____	

Tuesday   Total _____
             Hot _____
             Cold _____	

Wednesday   Total _____
             Hot _____
             Cold _____	

Thursday   Total _____
             Hot _____
             Cold _____	

Friday   Total _____
             Hot _____
             Cold _____	

Saturday   Total _____
             Hot _____
             Cold _____	

Sunday   Total _____
             Hot _____
             Cold _____	

*Reproduce table to enlarge to provide more space to write.

CHAPTER THIRTEEN

The Ax Has Fallen: Protect Your Image and Income

Your Goal:
Anticipate, articulate, and act.

Prenuptial Agreement

Finding the Right Fit position is very exciting, something akin to encountering your true love. However, rational thinking, not emotion, must govern the terms of the offer, agreement, or contract you negotiate and sign. The level of the position, the size and industry of the employer, and your personal circumstances all can impact significantly on the agreed-upon terms. This is a critical time in your new relationship with your employer, one in which you must think ahead about the possibility of divorce before you accept the position. In the event that the "marriage" does end someday, determine *prior* to the marriage who is entitled to what. The primary reason for the dissolution of the marriage will have an effect on what you are entitled to receive.

Carefully think through your particular situation and what it is reasonable to ask the employer to include in your agreement. Remember that the more the employer wants to hire you, the better your chances are of negotiating a strong "goodbye" package. If you will be generating revenue for your new employer and have a strong track record of doing so, you can use this to reinforce your justification for what you wish to receive.

Protecting yourself in the work world may appear unnecessary to you, unless you have had a painful experience. My goal is to prepare you for what could be harsh and brutal realities, providing solutions to alleviate and prevent as much pain as possible. I want you to understand the realities of the work world and take the necessary precautions, so that you are not a helpless victim. You must be prepared to act. Now is the right time to ready yourself.

To illustrate the broad spectrum of what you can negotiate in a prenuptial agreement, I selected the story of a CEO. It's important for you to understand that the realm of negotiation is broad. What is appropriate for you to request will depend on the level of your position and the company with which you're negotiating. If you are a CEO or considering this for your next career move, the details of the next story are directly related to you. If neither situation describes you, then use the details of the negotiation to expand your knowledge base, and extract the relevant concepts and apply them to yourself.

Now, let's look at a CEO, whom I'll name Michael, and how he approached negotiating for the future, before accepting a new position. Michael headed an East Coast biotechnology company with 700 employees, which he grew from 200 in only a few years. Following his passion for growing smaller companies, he decided to accept an offer to head a promising but ailing West Coast biotechnology company that had pursued him. They wanted him to make the company healthy, with the ultimate goal of going public. Michael was not unhappy in his current position, but the challenge of a "turnaround" intrigued him. Michael, like Ned, is a doer. He envisions that he can orchestrate significant growth, for which he wants to be rewarded.

Michael created a five-year plan, one that included his scenario for taking the company public. His performance benchmarks were integral to the plan because Michael would later tie them to his compensation. He presented the plan to the board, and the board was impressed. Shortly thereafter, the negotiating between Michael and the chairman of the board began. Let me highlight the key points that Michael negotiated for his "golden parachute," the crème de la crème of "goodbye packages."

Relocation

Michael had a wife, four children, and a five-bedroom home to relocate. The "new" employer agreed to:

- pay the closing costs for the sale of his home;

- fly him back to the East Coast every weekend for a full year, or until the house was sold;

- move his entire household, including his wine cellar, paying for packing and unpacking of all goods;

- cover all storage costs up to a year for his entire household, with special handling of the wine cellar;

- provide temporary housing for up to eighteen months for him and his family.

Michael negotiated a number of downsizing clauses, for example:

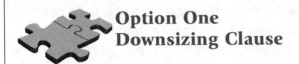

Option One
Downsizing Clause

In the event Michael is downsized for any reason other than performance or illegal or immoral acts, the employer will purchase the home from Michael at fair market value, if Michael and his family decide they no longer want the house. In addition, the employer will pay for relocation of Michael's entire household, including the wine cellar, back to the East Coast, or pay the cost for same, in the event that Michael chooses not to move.

Michael's focus on relocation and housing was very important. If he were to acquire a multimillion dollar home in Northern California, which he planned to do, he had to be very sure he could get rid of the home quickly, if he had to, and requiring his employer to purchase it took the burden off him. Inserting the clause to relocate him and his family to the East Coast or pay the cost of the relocation was clever. He and his family might, in the end, decide they prefer living in New Jersey; both he and his wife were born and raised in Cherry Hill, which they consider their home.

Compensation
Using the knowledge acquired from his Wharton MBA to full advantage, Michael carefully structured and negotiated a handsome compensation package. The new employer agreed to pay:

- a sign-on bonus of $50,000, payable on start date;
- a base salary of $500,000;
- a total performance bonus of $250,000 if all benchmarks are achieved in year one, with stated increases over a five-year period. In the event that all annual benchmarks are not achieved, one half of the total performance bonus will be paid for each year as long as Michael succeeds in achieving what the board labels as the "big three benchmarks." In the event that Michael fails to achieve the "big three" in year one, he will be fired and not entitled to exercise option one. Otherwise, option one stands.

Notice that in option two, Michael articulates the devil's details:

Option Two
Downsizing Clause

In the event that Michael is downsized after year one for any reason other than performance or illegal or immoral acts, he will receive $750,000, paid in two payments. The first of $500,000 within fifteen days after he is downsized, and the second of $250,000 three months from the date of downsizing. In year three, $800,000 and $300,000; year four, $850,000 and $350,000; and year five and after, $900,000 and $400,000.

Michael negotiated a compensation package for five years, taking full advantage of his revenue-generating capabilities. He was not concerned about year six and beyond because he planned to use his entrepreneurial talents to start his own business after year five. From previous positions, he had amassed wealth from stock options, and had orchestrated private and public stock-option plans with this company as well.

What is important for you to take away from Michael's negotiation is that he anticipated potential downsizing and planned accordingly—as if it would truly happen. He knew when he accepted the position that the company was ailing. He believed that he could turn the company around but never made that assumption. That's why he inserted the downsizing clauses, which were simply two among many. He focused on protecting his income, understanding the consequences of downsizing to him and his family, particularly with a very large monthly home-mortgage premium to pay.

When you negotiate your offer, envision yourself in a downsized situation. Then, determine what you need to ask for now, not later. Focus on severance, retirement, and health benefits. Study the company's policies and procedures manual to determine what is implicitly or explicitly stated that relates to downsizing and/or other types of termination. Use that information to guide you. For example, what will become of your health benefits? Usually, this is explicitly stated. Perhaps you can negotiate extending them. This is not necessarily easy to do, but determine what can be done, especially if you have a pre-existing health condition. Remember, you have to plan ahead as if you will be downsized. It's easier to prevent than treat a difficult situation.

Prior to accepting a written offer, you may also want to consult with an attorney who specializes in labor law to determine what should be added to your offer letter to protect you and to obtain further clarification of the company's policies and procedures. The attorney can also assist you with what you need to know about how the laws in your state may affect you.

I want to make it clear that I'm not suggesting that everyone needs to consult an attorney prior to accepting an offer in writing. But you do need to educate yourself about downsizing because it is a common occurrence, and one of many ways to do so is to consult an attorney. In Michael's case, it was essential for him to get legal assistance because the agreement was long and complex. When I negotiate agreements similar to Michael's in my search practice, the candidate often concurrently consults with an attorney while I am negotiating the offer. Sometimes I deal directly with my client-employer's attorney to negotiate the offer. It makes good sense for the candidate to seek legal advice to reduce the risk of future problems. You should decide what's right for you.

First Month of the Marriage

It is unfortunate that we need to plan ahead for the possibility of downsizing. I live in Los Angeles, earthquake country, and must prepare for this natural event, one that I have repeatedly experienced. Planning ahead in advance of earthquakes has always proven effective for me. Look at downsizing in the same way.

During the first month of your new "marriage," bring to the office a small piece of carry-on luggage and leave it in your office. Why? In the event of immediate downsizing—in which you are asked to leave right then and there—you will be able to pack your personal belongings quickly. Don't assume that you will have time to go to your car and get the luggage. I once observed a small business in decline and told one of its managers, whom I will call Linda, that the red flags I saw seemed to announce imminent closing. But Linda did not heed my warning and recommendations to prepare for that event. The next thing she knew, she was gone, and she called me to say, "The owner of the company came into my office. He fired me on the spot and told me to leave immediately. He would not let me take anything with me."

Linda had been with the company for eight years. She had decorated her office with plants she purchased herself, and she had also brought in her own furniture. But she was never allowed back into the office to collect her property. As Linda's unfortunate situation proved, you never know when an unexpected "goodbye" will occur. Be prepared. If Linda had followed my suggestions, she could have moved herself out of the office, prior to the ax falling.

Please note that you cannot take anything with you that is the property of the employer. With only a moment's notice, you would pick up nothing more than your personal possessions, such as plants, photographs, and art objects, which I recommend keeping to a minimum. Better yet, if you convince the employer to participate in decorating your office, then the bulk of the possessions will belong to the employer, and you won't be concerned about leaving them behind.

What else should you do to be prepared in case the ax falls? Keep all your personal papers at home. Maintain an active list of professional contacts on your personal computer so you can quickly send them an e-mail message explaining your departure. And be sure to create a list of business addresses and phone numbers in addition to the e-mail addresses; you may need them all.

Search your memory. Did you sign a non-compete agreement as part of your "prenuptial" employment package? And should you have thought about this beforehand? Absolutely. Find answers to these questions: Are you allowed to contact clients you met on the job? Does the reason for the downsizing have any impact on whether you can contact these people when you leave your current position? These issues need to be addressed at the time of the prenup, not after, just as Michael did. He knew he was planning to leave the new employer after five years. He persuaded the chairman of the board to agree to limit the time period of the non-compete in relation to the number of years he served as an employee. The result was that the specified number of years for the non-compete changed over time. Additionally, the company agreed to limit the non-compete to a specific geographic region. Planning ahead paid off for Michael, as you will see shortly, and can pay off for you as well.

The Ax Has Fallen

The first question to ask yourself is: Who is holding the ax? Again, make no assumptions. Are you, the employer, or both of you holding the ax? Let's find out, because there are several possible scenarios:

- If your employer downsizes a group of employees to save money and you are one of those employees, it's possible that both of you are holding the ax, depending on your role and function and your prenup.
- If your employer wants to downsize rather than fire you, then both of you are holding the ax. Remember Sabrina, who figuratively threw herself in a ditch? She and her employer were holding axes, which I will tell you more about, shortly.
- If your company has decided to outsource the function you are performing, then the employer may turn over the responsibility of downsizing to that firm, which now holds the power. If your prenup addresses this type of situation, you may have some recourse. In the case of an immediate dismissal that requires you to leave, as Linda did, recourse is not easy. That's why you must be ready to pack your bag quickly and go.

- If a conglomerate or a "wannabe" conglomerate purchases your company and downsizes you, there are ways to protect your image and your income, if you know how to proceed, and as long as you have some lead time to act. In this case, both you and the employer may be holding the ax.
- If the role is reversed and your company is purchasing another company and you are downsized, there are possibilities to win some privileges and more. Both you and the employer may be holding the ax.
- If, for whatever reason, you resigned, but the employer treats you as if you were suddenly "let go," that situation must be corrected. You must protect your image and income.

In order to prevent an employment situation that may be difficult to treat, which could require you to hire an attorney to assist you, it's critical to do the following:

- Plan ahead before you formally accept the position. Pay attention to the prenup as well as your company's policies and procedures. Seek legal advice, if necessary. Do what is necessary to protect yourself before the ax has fallen.
- While you are working, keep your ear to the ground and eyes peeled for red flags. Observe and listen, never ignoring the telltale signs of impending changes. In some situations, those changes can be beneficial. Change does not necessarily mean you will be downsized. Something good could happen to you. In fact, this is what Patti Rager noted about a major change at Nursing Spectrum:

There were two defining moments that accelerated our development as a company.

In 1994, Nursing Spectrum was sold to Gannett Company, Inc., a global Fortune 500 company whose business is newspapers, broadcasting, and interactive services. They are best known as the publishers of *USA Today*, the nation's largest newspaper. *When the surprise announcement was made, I was the first to blurt out, "What does this mean?"* Everyone was concerned about what would happen to our family-like entrepreneurial company, and *we all had the "me" question: "What does this mean for me?"* I began getting excited calls from advertising agency friends who said this purchase was a great thing. I soon realized the purchase was a good deal for Nursing Spectrum, as well as Gannett. With Gannett, our employees were eligible for much better benefits, and Gannett had the resources to invest in better technology and in acquisitions for Nursing Spectrum's growth. They also enabled us to do more philanthropy and to support important nursing causes.

After the acquisition, Patti rose to become president and publisher, and then chairman. She knew how to work with change, identifying the significant benefits that a large conglomerate could provide to the employees of Nursing Spectrum.

You and the Employer Negotiate

Let's look at how two employees Managed the Process in different ways when the ax fell, beginning with Sabrina, who was an executive assistant to the president of a public relations firm.

As you may remember, when I first introduced you to Sabrina, she was unemployed and working diligently to lose more than fifty pounds. She referred to the position from which she had been fired as a "pressure cooker," one that she endured for two years. Sabrina often worked eleven-hour days, then would work more when she arrived home, using her remote connection to her office computer. The president of the company traveled constantly from one country to another, and Sabrina worked nonstop to make all the travel arrangements. She scheduled conference calls at a moment's notice for fifteen to twenty people, making contacts across six to eight time zones. She responded to at least 300 e-mail messages a day. To add to her workload, Sabrina often was required to replace the BlackBerry devices and cell phones that her boss continually misplaced, and to help her work her way out of fenderbender auto accidents and other regular calamities. One time, the president was so distracted that her cashmere coat caught on fire while she was checking into a hotel. For whatever reason, the hotel had lit candles on the check-in desk, and the coat went up in flames.

Needless to say, Sabrina's work situation was difficult, and she had become increasingly unhappy. The company was also unhappy, but Sabrina did not understand why. A representative from the human resources department told her that she was "unable to represent the office in an appropriate way." Sabrina asked her to explain what that meant, but didn't get an answer. "They would give me a raise, and then tell me that I was in trouble. They gave me mixed messages, but I never got one from my boss." As Sabrina's unhappiness increased, she confided in a co-worker, who then informed her employer. Poised with ax in hand, the director of the human resources department called Sabrina into his office. "It became combative and ugly. We started to fight. The employer said, 'It's probably best that you leave.' I agreed to leave. They gave me their terms. I gave them mine. They accepted my terms, which I call an 'aggravation package.' They paid me all my vacation days for two years, personal days, bonuses, and six weeks of salary. They allowed me to collect unemployment. And they agreed not to say anything negative to my references."

When you are unhappy in a position and know that you can't fix it, do not delay, as Sabrina did. She brought the situation to a head by confiding her unhappiness to a co-worker, who immediately brought it to the attention of the employer. Let me repeat myself: *Trust No One.* There are lots of employees who believe they should function as "instant messengers."

 **Employer's Perspective**

When the employer gives you a vague message relating to your performance that you can't understand, refusing to clarify that message yet concurrently increasing your salary, you must understand what this means. The employer is informing you that he does not like you, but also acknowledges that your performance is excellent. What does not liking you mean? Simply that you do not fit in, for whatever reason.

If the employer accepts all your departure terms, as he did in Sabrina's case, this is a bit unusual. He is communicating the message that he wants you to leave without making waves. Because of her proximity to the president, Sabrina possessed a significant amount of personal and confidential knowledge that the employer did not want her to disclose. But the employer wanted her out the door immediately.

The list of terms to which the employer agreed clearly illustrates how Sabrina protected both her image and income. The company agreed to say nothing negative to references about her and accepted her monetary requests. Sabrina certainly would agree that she doesn't want another "aggravation package." In your own case, understand the significance of red flags, articulate what needs to be said when you observe the employer's discontent with you, and act accordingly. It's vital to prevent a situation similar to Sabrina's whenever you can.

Here's another example of how an employee handled the ax. I placed a candidate, whom I'll call Marsha, in a director-level position in the corporate headquarters of a for-profit company. Prior to her first day of work, I alerted her that she needed to move slowly and cautiously in this new culture, like a turtle. We both knew she posed a threat to one new colleague in particular, and we discussed how to handle this situation. Then, we talked about the differences between this for-profit organization and the not-for-profits where she previously had been employed. I also helped her understand that she needed to build relationships at her new company from the very beginning.

In the following months, I spoke intermittently with Marsha, and she said all was well. But after six months, Marsha called to ask my advice. She explained that my client-employer had financial problems, planned to modify her duties and responsibilities, and make her supervisor the person to whom she had posed a threat. Marsha told me she did not want to report to that person, but I explained to her that sometimes we all have to do what we don't want to do, at least for the short term. I told her exactly what to do to preserve her image and income, which included accepting lower-level duties and responsibilities and reporting to the person to whom she did not want to report, like it or not. I warned her that, if she did not agree to their terms, the company would let her go immediately, and Marsha agreed to follow my instructions.

But what did Marsha actually do? She took her own advice rather than mine, and the employer said good-bye to her immediately thereafter. Why give up a high-paying position because of ego? Please don't do what Marsha did. She was suddenly unemployed for no reason. She handed the ax to the employer and figuratively asked the company to chop off her head.

 **Employer's Perspective**

My client-employer purposely asked Marsha to accept tasks and responsibilities she did not want, betting that she would *not* accept the company's terms. If she would not accept those terms, she had two choices: resign or wait to be fired. Marsha resigned.

The approach my client-employer took demonstrated to me that Marsha's performance was excellent, perhaps too good. The company wanted her out of the limelight. Marsha accommodated them, but to her significant detriment.

I'm pleased to report, however, that I have experienced only one situation like Marsha's in my career. She didn't do what I asked her to do in the early months of her new position, and she failed to recognize the red flags around her. She didn't successfully protect her image or her income, wrongly believing she was doing so by not accepting a lower-level position. Instead, now Marsha was unemployed. What kind of image is that?

How to Protect Your Image and Income—
Ask, Ask, and Ask

I can't emphasize enough the importance of creating an amicable relationship with your employer. This relationship makes it possible for you to ask for—and often get—what you want in the event of downsizing or a reorganization that could lead to downsizing. Let me show you the steps.

- Accept another position at a lower level, at least for the short term, if you have this option. Depending on the company's internal circumstances, pitch yourself for another position. You might even identify an unrecognized need and then design and pitch a new position for yourself. Be open to suggesting new solutions. It is not uncommon for companies to downsize and then begin hiring again.

- Sometimes, it's possible to extend the timeframe for leaving that is stated in your downsizing letter. Discuss, for example, completing unfinished work the employer may want and need, requiring you to stay another month or two, perhaps three. Also, pursue the possibility of continuing with the company as a consultant, rather than an employee, which saves the company money.

- Determine carefully the money you should receive. Do not assume anything. Arrange a time to meet with a representative from the human resources department or someone who performs these functions. Prepare a list of questions and expectations. Include: severance, retirement, unemployment, bonuses, vacation, personal days, etc. Your goal is to collect as much money as you can to cover your expenses while you are searching for a new position. If you have decided to become an entrepreneur, you'll need this nest egg to support your new endeavor. Carefully review your prenup and the company's policies and procedures, as well as the notice of downsizing. Be assertive but not combative.

■ Request keeping your office voice-mail for at least a month after you leave to allow enough time for you to make "hot" and "cold" calls to your contacts. Maintaining the voice-mail will help protect your image, but it's important to change the message. Simply say: *"This is Harold Holiday. Please call me on my new direct line,"* *and state the phone number.* That new number should be your cell phone, unless you have a home phone that no one else answers. It isn't necessary to say anything more. Your goal is to catch the calls and explain later.

■ Request the installation of an automatic response for each e-mail message you receive for a month or more, which would say: *"Please e-mail me at hholiday@yahoo.com."* This approach will enable the employer to prevent you from reading information that could be confidential, but, at the same time, the person who sent the message will be able to reach you. This approach is a win-win-win situation for you, the employer, and the sender. If you have a strong relationship with the employer, he may agree to send you a list of the e-mail addresses of all the people who send you messages during the specified period, allowing you not to miss any e-mail contacts. As with

voice-mail, the continuance of e-mail can be
an effective way to protect your image.

■ Request that for a month or more the receptionist and/or your assistant provide your cell
phone number to your incoming callers. Hearing,
"She is no longer with us," does not protect your
image. The caller may think you were fired.

Protect your image and income, never taking anything
personally. It's just business, as they say. Believe it and behave accordingly.

What happened to Michael? His planning paid off. After
five years, he left the northern California company, moved back
to Cherry Hill, New Jersey, and started his own enterprise,
using his performance bonuses as seed money.

What do I wish for you? I hope that using the Right Fit
Method will make all your career dreams come true. *Remember, always compete with yourself and never against others.
Constantly change to reach higher and higher standards of
excellence.*

Together we're now ready to explore something new—
how to apply the Right Fit Method to your personal life, something that can bring immeasurable happiness to you.

Trigger Tip
Focus on the end result,
not your ego

Let's soar to new heights!

ACT IV

The Right Fit Method and You

CHAPTER FOURTEEN

The Right Fit:
An Approach to Life

Your Goal:
Find the road to happiness.

Looking at Yourself
Through an Airplane Window

Let's embark on a different sort of journey, one on which we'll explore the ways in which you view the totality of your life. Visualize yourself seated in a window seat on a sleek airliner ready for takeoff. Look out the window. As the plane begins to climb, imagine that you see yourself on the ground. From above, you can see yourself clearly and can examine the inner workings of yourself far below. The person standing on the ground is the person you are right now. The person ascending in the airplane is the person you will become—fulfilled, full of pride, and holding the keys to a happy life. You now have the necessary tools to integrate the Right Fit Method in your professional life. But this will require additional changes and soul-searching. Yes, probing deeply within yourself can be uncomfortable; but trust me, it will be worth the discomfort. After you discover what's really important to you, I'll show you how to become balanced and happy, the Right Fit Way.

I regularly observe many people who are out of balance. They can't identify their personal priorities. Yet, everything can't be of equal importance; if you don't differentiate among priorities and weight the importance of each priority, you'll be scurrying around like a mouse. You'll be busy but not productive.

Think about it. How many people are busy but accomplish very little? If you're one of them, then I will show you how to change that pattern of behavior. If you're productive, but not satisfied with your level of productivity, I'll show you how to accomplish your goals. Notice that the words I use are usually associated with professional, rather than personal, achievement. But from my perspective, it's all the same. It's critically important to apply the Right Fit Method to both.

To assist you in your professional life, you created more than one Blended Blueprint. Now it's time to apply the same concept to your personal life. If you are highly organized at work, functioning productively to achieve your goals, that's wonderful. If you arrive home and your life is chaotic because you haven't applied the same precision to managing your personal life, then you're adding needless stress and are on the road to unhappiness.

How can you pursue your personal life if you haven't clearly articulated your priorities? How can you select a life partner if you haven't determined how much time and effort you want to devote to that person? Determining whether to have children should be based on rational decisions and priorities. Otherwise: "*Oops*, I have four children! What do I do *now*?" At Harvard, students take a course titled "Happiness 101," which is designed to teach them how to build and maintain their happiness. And the way to achieve happiness is simple: Determine what's important to you. Once you do, then begin to search for "Right Fits" in every aspect of your life.

Begin to Balance the Whole Person

The first decision to make is how you choose to balance your professional and personal lives. It's very interesting that many women, married and unmarried, now rank their career as their highest priority.

Today, many husbands play the role of "mother," agreeing, whether through discussion or acquiescence, that their wife's career comes first, and assuming the primary role of raising the children. I know many couples who discussed the significance of their careers prior to marriage. Those men who agreed to put their future wife's career first consciously made the decision that their focus would be family, not career. The wives were happy because they have the best of both worlds—career and children. The agreement about balancing careers and personal lives sets the stage for a Right Fit marriage.

What happens if the career discussion does not take place prior to marriage? Challenges often arise. If assumptions have been made and not discussed, then the seeds of discontent have been planted—a discontent that can lead to divorce. For example, if the wife spends most of her waking hours working, how does her husband feel when she places him second to her career? Or third place, if there are children? Sometimes, the husband's place is *fourth*, after the wife's career, the children, and the pets. If the husband believes that his place in the family is at the very bottom of his spouse's priorities, he may look elsewhere for companionship.

Another example: What if the husband is suddenly fired, but his wife has a high-powered position and will not relocate to accommodate her husband? Who must move to take the Right Fit position? For their marriage to continue working, they must agree on a solution. The husband could agree not to relocate, or relocate himself, flying back on weekends to visit his wife and children. I have seen both solutions work effectively.

Now, I want you to answer this question for yourself: What is the relative importance of my personal life to my professional life?

You may decide that they are of equal importance. If so, then each would be weighted 50 percent. If one is more important than the other, then determine its proportional weight. For example, you might weight your personal life 75 percent and your professional life 25 percent, or vice versa. If you have to study the matter to respond, you are not in touch with yourself. Look at yourself through the window of the plane and quickly reach a conclusion. Be honest with yourself. The percentages should reflect honestly how *you* feel.

WEIGHT YOUR LIVES	
Personal Life	_____
Professional Life	_____
Total	<u> 100% </u>

What is the significance of the weights? They show you the direction you should take in your life. For example, if you assigned 80 percent to your personal life and 20 percent to your professional life, you have made a conscious decision to concentrate on your life outside your career. On the other hand, if the weights are reversed, you want to focus on your professional life. If you gave both equal weight, then you need to be highly organized and efficient to maintain the balance.

The assignment of weights should have a positive impact on how you feel about yourself. If you have been struggling with the balancing of your two lives, you now have a conscious direction to pursue. It would not make sense, for example, to buy a business requiring you to work sixty or more hours a week if you assigned your personal life a 70 percent proportion and your professional life 30 percent. It's important to make rational decisions based on those proportional percentages, decisions that are observable in the actions that you take. Consciously use the proportions to guide you in making decisions in the future.

Now it's time to assign weights to the components of your personal life in order to determine which to focus on as you create the Right Fit. I'll list some components and you can supply the rest. Keep in mind that you want to identify only the major components, and I strongly recommend that you don't weight each one equally. It's important to prioritize them so it's clear what's more important and less important to you. This will help you make decisions about your personal life as we proceed.

THE BLENDED BLUEPRINT	
Weighting	**Criteria**
_____	Career
_____	Life Partner
_____	Children
_____	Parents
_____	Siblings
_____	Friends
_____	_____
_____	_____
_____	_____
_____	**Total (100%)**

Review your weightings. Are you ready to Manage the Process in your personal life according to these priorities? For example, if "life partner" is your first priority, does your behavior reflect this? Be honest with yourself. If your career comes first, then weight that accordingly. If you have a life partner, he or she must concur with your weighting in order for the two of you to have a Right Fit relationship. If you are searching for a life partner, on the other hand, be sure to make your priorities clear when you find that person.

Use these weightings to guide you in managing the process in your personal life. Review them annually and modify, as necessary. The road to happiness is in your hands.

Home Grown: The Process and The Product

A chubby six-year-old girl with long, chestnut-colored corkscrew curls walked proudly, hand in hand with her dad, through the streets of Brookline, Massachusetts, the birthplace of John F. Kennedy. Her father, the cantor of a synagogue, seemed to know everyone. He would greet and talk to person after person. The little girl listened to every conversation intently while playing with her curls. After each conversation, her father asked his daughter, "What did we say?" He did not want her to recall the words that were exchanged, but the meaning behind the words. He wanted her to explain "with whom her dad was dealing," so she would never miss the "real" message. Throughout her adulthood, he continued to teach her the most important lesson of her life: You must understand "with whom you're dealing."

I was that little girl and the cantor who taught me was my dad. And his lessons did not stop with analyzing conversations. At age seven, I told my dad that I was planning to run away from home. I can still hear the torrents of rain beating on the roof of our house on the scheduled day of my departure. What did my dad do? He helped me pack my little pink suitcase. He dressed me in my matching pink raincoat and hat. Then he handed me my umbrella and stepped back. I walked to the front door and peeked out, observing the flooded streets. Then, I simply closed the door quietly. My dad and I never discussed what happened. He knew "with whom he was dealing," and that I was too intelligent to leave.

At age ten, my dad told me I had executive ability. He gave me a stack of bills and his checkbook, and showed me how to fill in the amounts so I could pay each bill. I immediately got to work. When my dad came home, he asked to see the checks. I told him I signed his name to each check, stuffed and stamped the envelopes, and mailed the checks. Astounded, he laughed. He erroneously assumed that I would only fill in the amount of each payment because that was all he had taught me how to do. He forgot that he had taught me a more important lesson as well—to understand the "real" message. That's why I finished the job for my dad, to save time for his personal pleasure.

He expected the bank to return the checks to him and couldn't believe it when the bank did not recognize that the signature on the checks was not his. They never did! He proudly reported to my aunts and uncles that he had found an executive assistant—his ten-year-old daughter.

My dad was the Right Fit for me. He knew how to mentor me using his own method to help me function effectively in a complex world using highly developed interpersonal skills. The ultimate outcome: I was successfully home-grown to succeed.

The person you are and the people your children become depend enormously on parenting. Did you have the Right Fit parent or parents? Perhaps one was and the other was not. If both were, you were blessed. In the event that you have issues stemming from unsuccessful parenting, you must overcome them. Remember the two brothers, one of whom was nominated for the Nobel Prize, while the other kept complaining about the wrong fit parents? Let go of the past parenting experiences that made you unhappy and treasure what made you happy.

If you are a parent now or planning to become one, start thinking about how best to interact with your children to become a Right Fit parent.

When you read Jason's story in chapters six and twelve, I hope it piqued your curiosity about his childhood. It did mine, and I asked him to write about his parents. Here is the conclusion to Jason's story.

My mom was never happy with my report cards. Not my grades, but my effort. I got straight As, but I always received "Unsatisfactory" marks for effort. I didn't need to try hard to get a good grade, so I didn't. It bothered me that my mom was more impressed with my younger brother's Cs, because he got an "Outstanding" in effort.

It took me a while, but in eleventh grade I finally figured it out. She wanted to see me give my best in anything I did, regardless of the outcome. On the other hand, I was only focused on the results and didn't care how I got there. I had never endured failure, so I didn't understand the value of effort, but my first Advanced Placement U.S. History test changed that. Without studying, I took my first test of the year and got a D. I didn't know what to do. Everything came so naturally in the past, but now the right answers weren't so obvious. Emily Dickinson once wrote, "Success is counted the sweetest by those who never succeed." This poem rang in my ears the whole first semester, as I had to work really hard to dig myself out of the hole I was in. With a little determination, I aced the rest of the exams and finished the semester with an A, but, more importantly to my mom, with an "Outstanding" in effort. She finally praised me for my report card. It was nice to hear. I continued this new idea of "trying hard" because I didn't want the bitterness of failure to bite me again. When I was awarded my valedictorian medal at graduation, my mom's tears of joy were what made me the proudest.

My dad also had a profound impact on my upbringing. When I was fifteen, he cut me off. No more allowance, no more cash for the movies. Nothing. I had to go out and get a job, if I wanted spending money to go out with my friends. I got a job at Mr. Philly's, cooking cheese-steaks, and the manager instilled in me a solid work ethic that would serve me well in my career. I became an assistant manager and was responsible for inventory, as well as cashing out the register at the end of my shift. I had a lot of power for someone so young, so I tested the limits by bringing my homework to the restaurant and doing it during my shift. This was a bad call, as the manager caught me slacking off from the job to work on my trigonometry homework. My dad also taught me to take responsibility for my actions, so when I went in to meet with the manager later in the week and he fired me, I understood completely.

I went in the next Saturday to pick up my final paycheck and the manager was understaffed and overwhelmed with customers. I had never seen the place so busy. He told me that my check was in the back and I grabbed it, but before I left, something drew me back to the kitchen. "Do you need some help?" I asked, and I spent the next two hours cooking up a storm to help with the rush. After the steady stream of customers had been served, I said my goodbyes and began to leave. "Wait a minute," my manager said, "You just earned your job back." From that day forward, I never took advantage of an employer and always understood the consequences of my actions.

My dad was also a good golfer, not a great golfer, but a good one. Yet, every year when his golf club had its championship tournament, he would play in the highest bracket with all of the semi-pro golfers, rather than in the middle bracket, which he would have had a good shot at winning. When I asked him why, he told me that if you're not going to play for all the marbles, don't play at all. What fun was it to win a tournament if you only won your little subset? *Go big, or go home.* I took that lesson to heart and never accepted success unless it was deserved. I held myself to this high standard throughout sports, academics, and eventually business.

Jason was home-grown to succeed. His mother stressed effort; his father, self-reliance. He figured out the meaning, significance, and value of his parents' messages. If Jason had not been really smart and had not "got it," he could have become angry and rebellious. His parents understood "with whom they were dealing."

Learn who your child is and tailor your mentoring method so you, too, will become Right Fit parents. If your mentoring messages and broadcast style are the wrong fit for your child, you will not achieve the desired result—a happy child who can function successfully, both personally and professionally. It's up to you to Manage the Process—interacting with your child—appropriately.

How do Jason and his wife Jennifer interact with their two-year-old, blue-eyed son Sam? They focus on teaching Sam how to be rational, using sequencing as the method. For example, Sam goes to sleep after his dinner, bath, and story. According to Jason, Sam never fusses about going to sleep because he knows the sequence of events that will occur each evening.

Jason selected a Right Fit spouse as well. "I picked her because she was rational," he explained. With two rational parents, Sam will learn not only rationality, but also consistency, because both parents communicate the same messages, consistently.

A twenty-four-year-old graduate of Yale University's prestigious School of Drama, whom I'll call Rieley Hardt, takes center stage, sharing her story and describing how she was home-grown and the challenges she faced.

My mother's family is from Jamaica and Panama; my father's from Holland, Canada, and St. Croix. My parents didn't want my fourteen-year-old sister to be an only child, so they tried for many years to have a second child before my mom was finally able to get pregnant with me. Sometimes, my parents joke and call me "the miracle baby" because my mom was in her fifties. I arrived a week late and on my dad's birthday. Who could ask for a better present?

My childhood was a time of fun and innocence, yet when I did push the limits, my parents disciplined me, gave me an allowance, chores, and assigned curfews. They also empowered me, giving me responsibilities, and good grades got me additional freedoms. My parents always let me know that, no matter what, we'd never lose the open line of communication between us.

Growing up in New York City, I had a great childhood. I had friends, participated in different activities, attended parties, and went to the theater and museums. Then, we moved to Holland for a few years, and that was fun too. In Holland, my friends were pretty international—one day I'd go to a friend's house and we would have Korean food, another day we would have Ethiopian food. Then, we'd come to my house and have Caribbean and Dutch food. At the time, it was just what we did. However, now I realize how valuable it was to learn about so many different cultures.

One day, when I was seven years old, I auditioned for the dance school ballet recital. Some kids were really competitive and mean to me. One tried to trip me. I ran crying to my mom. When I finished crying, she told me there was no room for cowards in our house. It is okay to be scared, she said, but you do the scary thing anyway because you are a worthy human being of good character. Only later on did she confess that she was so worried about what would happen to me that she stayed and watched in the back of the audition room.

I asked Rieley what she did after her mother discussed cowardice with her. *She said she went back to the audition and stood her ground. She did not go to the back of the auditorium, which was what the kids wanted her to do. Instead, she stood in the front, tuned the kids out, and focused on her dance steps.* Many years later, she would respond similarly in a situation that was potentially dangerous. Rieley went on to describe her mother in detail.

My mom is a fabulous woman, a retired psychologist, easy going, warm, kind, compassionate, yet straightforward. Don't ask her opinion unless you really want the truth, and she doesn't believe in limitations.

My mother created a world for me without limits. She wanted my sister and me to be the best people we could be. She would work very hard as a psychologist but still make time to spend with us. She would fix a meal and invite our friends to the house and spend time getting to know them. She always felt it was important to know her daughters' friends. My mother showed me I had the potential to become anything I wanted to be. She always offered us aphorisms like, "If you're going to step up to the bell, ring it." "Adjust to changing times but cling to unchanging principles." "You are more important to yourself than you think you are." "If anything's worth doing, it's worth doing well."

She also said, "Life is not a dress rehearsal." At the end of life, she told me, you will never regret not having passed one more test, not buying one more car, winning a team sport, or not closing one more deal. However, you will regret time not spent with family and friends. Not celebrating enough of the bountiful pleasures of life. If something is in your control and you have committed yourself to it, you must step up to the plate and bat. However, when something unexpected happens that's beyond your control, you must trust that whatever you need will come to you at the right time.

One day, when I was in my early teens, my mother planned a special "girls day" for just the two of us. "Girls day" usually meant we would go shopping. I would pick where we'd eat, and we would go to a movie. It was always a lot of fun. It was her way of spending quality time with me. But this time was different. My mom and I got all dressed up and went for tea at the Plaza Hotel. That's when she told me about life and love and tried to talk about serious things, like my becoming a woman someday. She tried to speak to me about sex. Because I was embarrassed to discuss such matters with my mother, I quickly said, "Don't worry, I know everything." Then, my mother said, "If you know everything, then the rest of your life is going to be boring," which got my attention. "Life is about growing and learning from accomplishments as well as failures," she said. "Try to remember that we all do the same things— we eat, we sleep, we go to the bathroom, we work, we cry, we laugh, we make love—but what makes you different is how you do it." What I learned on that day is that I had to take responsibility for myself, and if I could do that, my life could be more than the things I did, it would be about *how* I did them.

Rieley's mother consciously taught her to function independently, to be an individual, and to embrace life to its fullest. But did she teach her to know when to say "no"?

Growing up in New York City, I was influenced greatly by my parents' love of the arts. My sister took piano lessons, and I took dance lessons. My parents always encouraged my sister and me to "think outside of the box." That's why it was so surprising to me when they didn't encourage my decision to become an actress. My parents wanted me to have a "serious profession," like a lawyer, doctor, etc. "Acting should only be a hobby," they said. They were aware of the ups and downs of the business and wanted me to avoid the heartache and rejection that so many people in the industry have encountered. But, of course, I looked at it as a challenge. I wanted to prove to them that I could do it. I thought they'd be unbelievably impressed. I think I had a little streak of rebelliousness, too. I didn't consider the hurtful end of it. I just knew that acting was a "natural high" for me, and I felt that I could contribute to society through acting. I also cared about making my family proud of me; it didn't really matter what other people might think I could or couldn't do.

The major turning point in my parents' acceptance of my dream was when, at eighteen, I was in a critically acclaimed off-Broadway play. I worked hard and when opening night arrived, we were well received. I received a rave review in the *New York Times,* which said I gave a "heart-wrenching performance" and I was a "young talent to watch out for." I was thrilled and my parents were very proud.

Rieley successfully convinced her parents—with help from the *New York Times* review—that she should pursue an acting career. She likely would never have enrolled in Yale's School of Drama, if her parents had not ultimately agreed that the career she wanted to pursue was the Right Fit for her. Her father and her sister proved as supportive as her mother.

My dad is a great man, a retired judge with a good sense of humor, great intuition, full of stories, a man who always thinks things through. Before I entered Yale, my dad said, "you'll be among the best of the best in school, just remember that you are not competing with them. They are your classmates. Treat them with respect. Set standards for yourself, compete with yourself, do the best that you can and you will succeed because looking over your shoulder to see what everyone else is doing is a waste of time and creates too much negative energy."

When I decided to go to Yale, my sister said, "You are very talented, charismatic, and you have that *joie de vivre* that it takes to be an actress. Just don't take critics and negativity to heart. There are many people who will try to stand in your way, even cut you off at the knees for whatever reason, but it is often much more about them than about you."

At Yale, Rieley followed her father's and sister's advice. *But had her parents or her sister adequately prepared her to handle what happened next?* She began dating a young man who initially appeared terrific. Then, she started to observe unusual behaviors in him that worried her and even frightened her.

He would call me at inappropriate times. Although I had dated before, this was the first time I had to give boundaries. I said to him, "I feel the need to set some boundaries with you, and I need for you to respect them." I had to give him time-calling boundaries from 10:00 a.m. to 10:00 p.m. Even with setting the time boundaries, my guidelines were ignored. He was a morning person, so he'd call at 6:00 a.m. or 7:00 a.m. to book a date for the weekend.

He'd repeatedly call between the hours of 10:00 p.m. and 2:00 a.m., not leave a message and slam the phone down when I didn't pick up, with each slam angrier than the next. He always wanted to know what I was doing and where I was going and with whom. He even wanted a copy of my class schedule. He'd lurk in the bushes on campus or by the apartment and pop out suddenly. It made me very paranoid.

He wanted to try to hypnotize me. He became more and more aggressive about trying to control me. He'd pick strange places to go on our dates. The last date was to a historical, out-of-the-way cave. Yes, that's right, a cave! But, in the end he ended up leaving the university and I had a fresh start.

After I read Rieley's description of the young man she dated, I probed her further to determine why she went on that third date, given the fact that she was terrified. She told me that even though she was now very afraid of the young man, she was a person of her word. She had told him she would go out with him and felt she could not change her mind. Did it also have something to do with not wanting to act like a coward? I asked. Remember what her mother told her at her audition years before—that there was no room for cowards in their house.

Rieley agreed that, yes, she had been reluctant to appear to be a coward. She knew with whom she was dealing—a wrong-fit date, whom she could not change—yet she continued to go out with him because of what her mother had taught her as a small child. It's critical to recognize when you should and should not act on the teachings of your parents. Luckily, Rieley's trip to the cave unfolded without incident, but it's an excellent example of what she *should not* have done. For someone who was raised in New York City, going to a play, a museum, or Central Park is the Right Fit. Visiting a cave was alien to Rieley. Even if her date did not have psychological problems, she should not have gone to the cave because it was the wrong-fit place for her to go. If it doesn't feel right, you shouldn't do it.

In child rearing, it is very important to differentiate among concepts that you are attempting to teach your children. If the concept is simple—*do not touch the stove, it is hot*—that's different from explaining about cowardice, which is an abstract concept. A small child sees things as either right or wrong. The capacity to judge only develops over time. To teach abstract concepts to the young, you must qualify the message, saying, for example, "It's important for you to assert yourself in different situations. Sometimes, it may be best not to assert yourself and just walk away." Give examples of those situations. Plant the seeds of judgment instead of attempting to teach the child to behave one way or another in every circumstance, an attitude that fosters rigidity and poor decision making.

When you're dating—at any age—identify the components of the Right Fit date, weighting the importance of each as you clearly identify your priorities. Be sure not to confuse the Right Fit date with the Right Fit life partner. Someone could be a very fun date, but not necessarily the Right Fit person to live with or marry. You might have great walks, talks, and sex, but that person might be unreliable, disappearing for long periods of time, then reappearing again with no believable explanation. Is this person the Right Fit for you over the long term? Watch the red flags and pay attention to them. Prevent a bad situation before you need to treat it.

I met Helen Hurst at a national meeting for nurse educators. While we were discussing *Win Without Competing!*, I asked her how she managed to juggle working on a doctoral degree, university teaching, two children, and a husband. She described her marriage to her husband Mike, and, when I learned that she still kept and treasured two diaries from their early years together, I asked her to share her intense and exciting courtship. Let's welcome onstage Helen, from Louisiana:

I was seventeen years old, and my father was working in the Middle East. My mom and I stayed at home in England so that I could continue in college, rather than attend a foreign school. My mom was a critical-care nurse, and my parents made the decision that my dad would work away from home three months at a time. During that summer, I stayed with some of my parents' friends in Saudi Arabia, as my dad only had a one-bedroom house. While there, I met someone, who would change my life forever.

Sitting by the pool one day in the American compound, I met a group of American helicopter pilots. One in particular was exceptionally handsome and funny, although he was obviously a little older than me. I thought that he must be about twenty-three or twenty-four. We talked on and off and I was attracted to him, but there was nothing overtly romantic about it. We visited daily, and I learned a lot about him. He was, in fact, eighteen years older than I was, had a son my age, and was separated from his wife. I was shocked, and I immediately shelved any romantic illusions I had conjured up. However, sometimes you don't get to choose whom you like and whom you don't. When I left Saudi Arabia that summer, we decided to write to each other on a platonic basis only.

Beginning in September, we wrote to each other daily, and I really mean daily. I still have every single letter and card he ever sent to me. It soon became apparent to both of us that we really missed seeing each other. He told me all about being married and a father at seventeen, about his experiences in the Vietnam War, and the strained relationship he had with his wife. In turn, I no doubt bored him with the everyday trials of a seventeen-year-old in college.

During this time, I told myself I was crazy to write to someone who was eighteen years older than me, still married, and whom I never saw. I wrote him and told him we had no future and to stop writing. I think I cried as I wrote every word, but even then I think I knew deep down that I had found the person I wanted to spend the rest of my life with. I began to date again, but my heart wasn't in it. The boys I dated seemed like such *boys*, and it was all too much work.

The following summer, I was back in Saudi Arabia, and I had turned eighteen. The first day there, I went to Mike's apartment and left a note. "The English girl is back! Call me!" It would be a note that would change my life. For days I didn't hear from him, and I was devastated. How could I be feeling this way? We were not romantically involved; we had stopped writing. It just didn't make sense. Then, about a week later, I got a phone call from him, asking me to come to dinner. I thought I was going to faint. I had never been so nervous in my entire life prior to seeing him again, but the moment I saw him, he hugged me and I knew I didn't care what we had to endure, what obstacles we had to overcome, I was going to marry this man!

September came around and I had to go back to England. Again we started writing, and now we started calling, too. My parents were worried about what I was getting into. I was an only child and I think I was mature for my age, and I was blessed to have parents who supported me and gave me quiet advice, but who never pushed or demanded. I think they secretly thought, "He is thousands of miles away, and this will pass." How wrong they were! Every day I anxiously awaited the mail, and without fail there would be a letter or a card. We wrote about everything under the sun. I think we communicated more in those letters than anyone who dated face-to-face. We said what we felt; we laughed and cried. Long phone conversations also ensued, but every six weeks he would take a flight home to Texas and not to England to see me. The four weeks he would spend in the states were terrible for me—no letters, no phone calls, no contact. What is the point, I would think? And once my mom said, "I don't know why you want to pick bruised fruit anyway," referring to the fact that he was still not divorced.

One time, Mike came and stayed overnight at my parents' house, but after that it was eighteen months until I saw him again. The letters continued, but I was starting to feel like I was second in line, and I began to pressure him to make a firm decision about our relationship. So, after eighteen months, we decided to meet in Amsterdam and talk about our plans for the future. I can only imagine the mixed emotions my parents had about his trip, but as usual, they were quietly supportive. He and I had a fabulous time in Amsterdam, but we didn't really resolve anything.

By this time I was twenty, and in the fall I went on an exchange program from my university in England to a small liberal arts college in the heart of Pennsylvania. He came to England, and we traveled to the U.S. together. We flew to Houston, then drove to Pennsylvania. We spent two weeks on the road, and he showed me dozens of places along the way, and it was the most romantic and fun trip I had ever had. Once I was settled, he returned to Saudi Arabia, but not before renting an apartment in my college town where he planned to stay when he was in the U.S.

In October, I received a huge vase of flowers, with a note from him: "I did it." He had filed for divorce. That Christmas, my parents flew to Toronto, and we spent the holidays with my aunt and uncle. It had been years since the whole family had been together, and I had an engagement ring, although we were careful to keep it hidden. When he arrived from Saudi Arabia, he handed my dad a letter asking if he could marry me, explaining that we wanted to be married in the summer. My father said "yes," and my mother began to cry, saying, "I just didn't think this would happen so soon." To her, it was too soon, but for us it had been years.

I went back to college and my mom went back to England and planned my wedding. I went home in June, and Mike arrived a week before the wedding. On August 30, 1986, I could hardly believe it was real as I rode to the church. For many of my family and friends, this was the first time they would meet my husband.

Helen and Mike's story suggests that they were the Right Fit and perhaps even a flawless fit. But their life together grew far more complicated than she could ever have imagined. Helen explains:

On September 2, 1986, I turned twenty-one, on my honeymoon. In 1989, Maria was born, and in 1994, Madeline came along. So, where are we today? What has happened? Along the way, I finished my degree in business and a year later went back for my BS in nursing. Mike came back to the U.S. full time and went into management. I got my master's and became a certified nurse midwife, ultimately ending up where I am today, teaching obstetrics in one of the largest nursing programs in the country.

However, during the past twenty years, we have become lost to each other. The pressures of children, advancing careers, and juggling all of it have taken precedence over our relationship.

We have gone from being the great letter-writing communicators to people who just live in the same house. Who has time for romance and keeping a marriage alive and vibrant when there are always issues with the children, demanding jobs, and with me now trying to complete my doctorate? I talk with my friends, many of whom are nurses, and we all seem to be facing the same issues and challenges. Although we have built a wonderful network of friends, having all my family overseas has made finding help with the girls a constant worry. It is stressful for me if things don't run according to my plan. Even when I am away on business, the children call me to ask for advice, and I, in turn, call and check to make sure everyone is where they are supposed to be at the required times.

But our marriage takes a position at the bottom of the ladder. Time for each other just doesn't exist. As for communication, who has time for that? Mike goes to bed early because he goes to work early; I stay up late and work on projects because I am a night owl. We are both tired. I often wonder if we should start writing to each other again. On several occasions he has asked me, "I am at the bottom of your list, aren't I?" Although I don't want to admit it, I know he is right. I don't seem to have the time or the energy to work on a romantic relationship. I think this may sound familiar to many people. Our husbands take the back seat to everything that is going on in our lives. After all, they love us so much they let us pay them no attention. Is this the way I want things to be? Of course not. Would I do all this again with the same man? Absolutely, without question! I just don't know how to "fix" it.

What Do You Do with a Right Fit Marriage Gone Wrong?

When I talked with Helen after reading her story, I realized that Mike was the fourth priority in her life—after career, children, and even pets. I asked whether Mike had read those diaries she kept from their first years together. She said he had asked to read them more than once, but she had not let him. I told her the time was now. They were preparing for a Christmas cruise, and I suggested that she giftwrap the diaries, take them on the trip, and present them to him as a Christmas gift. She loved the idea and said she would do it. I knew Mike would see this gift as communicating an important message—*you are important to me, and I want to rekindle our romantic relationship.* Did this strategy work? Absolutely. The right gift is an effective way to pitch a message. Be thoughtful about determining and selecting the right gift for your life partner.

What does Helen need to do next, after they return home from the cruise? She must reorder her priorities so that she schedules quality time for Mike and herself in the same way she schedules everything else. Parents spend lots of time chauffeuring their children. Why not hire someone else to do part of that job, even though finding the Right Fit assistant may not be easy? Why not carpool your children to reduce the number of times you need to drive weekly? Manage the Process rather than becoming submerged in your responsibilities. This is an important step in maintaining a Right Fit marriage.

What does Mike need to do next? Mike travels a lot as the chief pilot of a large helicopter company. Sometimes, Helen doesn't know when he will be coming home or going away. He, like Helen, needs to Manage the Process better. When Mike understands that he is no longer Helen's fourth priority, he can determine how to travel less or take Helen with him some of the time.

Both Helen, age forty-one, and Mike, age fifty-nine, need to change their behaviors in order to reconnect and capture the romance and intimacy that is the Right Fit for them now, as it was long ago. They must arrange a time for a long conversation to Pick, Probe, and Pitch to fix their fit for their long-term future together.

Friendship is a significant ingredient in sustaining personal happiness, regardless of personal wealth. The two richest entrepreneurs in the world, Bill Gates and Warren Buffett, are the best of friends. When Gates met Buffett, he said, "I felt that I had met my match." They spent ten hours talking together on that first occasion, according to Gates. Sharing the same values is a major component of their match. Neither man flaunts, boasts, or ostentatiously exhibits his wealth. Buffett lives in Omaha, Nebraska, in the same home he bought forty-eight years ago for $31,500. At age seventy-six, he drives his own car. If you were to ask Buffett about hiring a chauffeur, he would say, "Why?" Demonstrating his strong belief in Gates's ability to use his wealth to make the world better, Buffett willed 41 billion dollars to the Gates Foundation. Buffett is committed to ethics as his number one priority in business, a priority that spilled over into his personal life. And by giving the majority of his wealth to the Gates Foundation, he made a profound statement about his belief in his friend's ethics as well.

Before you select a friend, think about the Right Fit components of the match. Remember Gates and Buffett.

My Right Fit Method is my gift to you—your key to unlocking the doors of fulfillment, pride, and lasting happiness. Balance your professional and personal lives. Always strive to select the Right Fit for every situation. Set stellar standards for yourself, competing with yourself, never against others. As Warren Buffett says, "I can't play the other guy's game."

Trigger Tip
The Right Fit Method: your lifetime companion

Let's carry on together!

CURTAIN CALL

I WANT TO THANK my storytellers again for sharing themselves and their lives onstage with you, and I want to ask them
to take a bow now. In order of appearance in *Win Without
Competing!*, here are:

Grace Tiscareno-Sato
Doyle Gray
Jason Moreno
Ned Hepner
Patti Rager
David Doran
William Ernest Brown
Rieley Hardt, and
Helen Hurst

ENCORE

I RECENTLY HAD A NOTE from Helen Hurst and was delighted to learn that she followed my advice and shared her courtship diaries with her husband Mike during their holiday cruise. She wrote:

Well, we went on our cruise, and, Arlene, I followed through with your suggestion to give Mike the diaries as a gift. Each day on the ship, I put it off. I couldn't find the right time. I mean, this was like giving away a piece of my soul; no one but me had ever seen them. But, on our last night I gave them to him, wrapped in a single box. When he opened the diaries, he was stunned. He said he was truly speechless and didn't know what to say. He was overwhelmed and couldn't believe I would give to him something so personal. He said it was as though I was giving him a piece of my soul. We were both tearful, and it brought us both back to how strong our emotions were before we were married. Marriage is work, everyone agrees, but sometimes we have to sit back and realize how it all started. I know Mike and I would do it all over again. We just need to remember that, and to keep in mind that we were a perfect fit long ago, and we remain the Right Fit today.

I'm delighted that my Right Fit Method worked for Helen, and I know that it will work for you, too.

EPILOGUE

I HOPE YOU HAVE BEEN enthralled by this production of *Win Without Competing!*—that it has inspired, motivated, enlightened, and entertained you. Now, it's your turn to stage a production of the Right Fit Method in your professional and personal lives as well. Use the tools that I have given you wisely.

Success, fulfillment, and happiness now lie in the palm of your hand. The world of *Win Without Competing!* lives on in you and me. I'm eager to learn about the experiences you have had implementing the Right Fit Method, and I would love to read *your* stories. Please go to my *Win Without Competing!* website and share your stories with me at www.winwithoutcompeting.com. When you submit your story, you will be eligible to join my Win Without Competing Club. My personal e-mail address is drbarro@winwithoutcompeting.com. Become a storyteller, one who steps onto the center of the stage in my next book.

We will carry on together!

Goodbye for now,
Dr. Arlene

INDEX

ABOUT
THE AUTHOR

"WIN WITHOUT COMPETING" is the life mantra of Arlene R. Barro, PhD, a nationally recognized search consultant and career coach who is an educator, educational psychologist, and evaluator. From UCLA, Dr. Barro holds a PhD in education with distinction for her doctoral dissertation on creativity. Her pioneering research monograph on measuring physician performance for the Association of American Medical Colleges changed the course of medical education throughout the world and led to her appointment as a visiting professor in the medical education department at Ben Gurion University in Israel. She served as a dean at the medical school of the State University of New York at Stony Brook and as a professor at Thomas Jefferson University's medical school in Philadelphia. At the National Cancer Institute (NCI), National Institutes of Health, Dr. Barro administered a $60 million public and professional education program, founded and directed the NCI's first educational research and evaluation branch, and envisioned and directed a first-of-its-kind national program to educate physicians and other health professionals about disease prevention, with a focus on cancer. She has served as the guest editor for professional journals, contributed articles on many topics, and was the creator of the Anti-Cancer Audiobook Series, recommended for the general public by the American Library Association.

Following a long career in the medical field, during which time she held a number of positions usually occupied only by physicians, Dr. Barro joined Search West, an established leader in the professional search industry, where she became director of the company's Healthcare Services Division, creating the Right Fit Method in response to the critical need she perceived to improve hiring and career-search practices in every business sector. Eight years later, she established barro global search, the firm she continues to lead. A colleague's admiring remark that, throughout her career, Dr. Barro has

Arlene R. Barro, PhD

"set a standard against which no one else can compete" is a truth that this Renaissance woman continues to live by. This high standard underscores her success in each of her career challenges and has enabled her to effect important and lasting innovation. And it is a core principle of the Right Fit Method, which continues to revolutionize the way in which candidates, employees, entrepreneurs, and employers successfully meet their career, business, and life goals.

Dr. Barro lives in Los Angeles.